HOW TO TRAIN
THE FAMILY DOG

by Willy Necker

PUBLISHERS • GROSSET & DUNLAP • NEW YORK
A FILMWAYS COMPANY

ISBN: 0-448-01498-X

1978 PRINTING

PRINTED IN THE UNITED STATES OF AMERICA

WILLY NECKER

For nearly 50 years Willy Necker has been one of the leading figures in obedience dog training in America. In the intervening time he has trained over 10,000 dogs, and the number is still expanding.

Necker's father, a building contractor in Stuttgart, Germany, raised dogs as a hobby. It was thus natural that son Willy should grow up with a deep interest in dogs. In his early teens he was spending all of his available time training the family dogs; for him this was the most interesting phase of owning the animals.

In 1929, at the age of 20, Necker came to America and soon found a place for himself in kennel work in Detroit, Michigan. He continued his training activities and was soon giving demonstrations of trained dogs at obedience contests, schools, fairs, clubs and other large gatherings. After a few years he moved to Wheeling, Illinois, a suburb of Chicago, and established his own kennel. Started in a small way, this has through the years been expanded until it is now the largest of its type in the United States. Rain or shine, summer or winter, dogs are continually being trained by Necker and his staff. Dogs are sent here from all parts of the country to be trained, according to their owners' orders, in obedience work, as watch dogs, as trick dogs, as well behaved companions or as expert gun or field trial workers. Willy Necker is often called upon to break various bad habits which have been acquired by fond owners' pets. An additional strong feature of Necker's "Canine University" is the course for hunting and retrieving dogs. He has many acres of his own over which the dogs can range as he schools them in their duties as hunting companions.

Necker held the rank of lieutenant commander in the U. S. Coast Guard during World War II. He was in charge of training War Dogs in the work of guard, messenger, and attack duties. Thousands of the animals were under his direction in these important fields.

As exhibitor of obedience trained dogs, licensed judge of obedience dog competitions, and handler of championship field trial dogs, Willy Necker has appeared before thousands of dog lovers throughout the country. Additional millions have seen him on many nationally televised shows putting his wonderfully trained Dalmatians and Doberman Pinschers through their paces. These exhibitions, coupled with sparkling displays of retrieving ability by Necker-trained hunting dogs, have been very popular at Sportsmen's Shows, fairs, theaters, clubs, schools, dog shows, and other large groups of spectators.

Willy Necker has been cited by the S. P. C. A. for the kindness he shows toward his pupils. His methods eliminate all cruelties occasionally associated with animal training; he has always substituted skill and knowledge of dog behavior for the more crude methods which are sometimes relied upon. Anyone who has seen his dogs in action can testify that they obviously love their master. Necker has always said that "a trained dog is a happy dog."

FOREWORD

A family dog is a wonderful possession. Few family belongings can give more pleasure than a dog. This is true in large families and small, for city dwellers and those in country circles. For thousands of years dogs have been the favorite animals on the domestic scene. All ages in the household enjoy the antics of the puppy and the companionship of the grown dog. The loyalty of the dog to his master is traditional.

But this pleasure is not without cost, and I do not mean the money cost of the dog and its upkeep. I mean the cost in time and effort in keeping the animal in good health, presentable in appearance, and obedient and well mannered in the home and in public.

Even though this book is primarily about training the family dog I have felt that a certain amount of information on the basic care of the animal should be given before serious training is discussed. A poorly fed dog cannot be successfully trained, nor can one that is not in a good state of health. If the dog has poor sleeping accommodations, if they are dirty, damp, too hot or too cold, or not large enough for comfort, he won't be able to get the proper amount of necessary rest. Such a dog would be tired, inattentive, and completely uninterested in training lessons.

If you are an experienced owner of family dogs, and know how to feed and house them, you will find it unnecessary to spend time reading about these subjects, and can start right in with the training, beginning on page 31. But if you are a new owner you should first become familiar with all of your duties in this field before attempting to teach your dog its place in society.

In addition to the care and training you give your dog to make him an acceptable member of your family group, there are other considerations of which you should be aware. These are the obligations, which you assume as a dog owner, toward your community, your neighbors, and every one who will come in contact with your dog. Your community has certain laws or ordinances regarding dogs; these you should become familiar with and respect. Your neighbors have certain rights of privacy which you must not allow your dog to violate; a dog allowed to run at large in the neighborhood can do a lot of damage. Passersby your home, people who visit your family, and every person coming in contact with your dog have the right of being safe from your dog; you are responsible.

A well behaved dog is a great pleasure to own; fortunately it is both easy and lots of fun to train one.

Even Necker's famous Dalmatian, Jitterbug, sometimes makes a mistake. But it makes him so ashamed of himself that he tries to hide his head from his master's gaze!

CONTENTS

No matter what breed you choose your pup will quickly make a place for himself in your family's routine — and its affections. The fun and entertainment that he will provide will more than make up for the work and care that he will require.

HOW TO CHOOSE A DOG

I am starting out by assuming that you are going to get, or already have, a puppy. Most dogs which are destined to be family pets go to their permanent homes as puppies. Actually the very fact that they *are* cute little pups is the thing that prompts their purchase. It would never occur to most people, having made up their mind to have a dog in their home, to start looking for a grown dog.

Most grown dogs change hands because the purchaser is looking for a dog for some very specific purpose other than that of a pet. A sportsman is very apt to buy a full grown bird dog, a trained one at that, so that he will not lose a precious year of sport. A person needing a watch dog is very likely to look around for a grown dog, and buy the fiercest one he can find. Other mature animals change hands because for one reason or another the first owner can no longer keep the dog and he prevails upon a friend to take him into his home.

I believe that the purchase of a puppy is the best plan for a family wanting a pet dog, but I do know that there are valid reasons for some households to start right out with an older animal. Chief among these reasons is the fact that it is possible to buy a dog which has already been trained. For some people the very thought of training a dog repels them. They do not realize that the training is half the fun of owning a dog. Some people are not tempermentally suited to train them. A few are not physically able to do their own training. For cases such as these it is wise to buy a grown dog — much wiser than to forego entirely the pleasures of having a pet dog in the home.

Buying a fully grown dog also gives the purchaser the exact knowledge of what he is getting, as far as size, conformation, and personality are concerned. This is of great value for the person looking for a show dog, for instance, but not too important for the family in search of a pet. If the latter buys a pure bred pup it will know pretty much what it will look like, what size it will attain, and what its personality will be like, by judging the mother and father dogs as well as the standards for the breed. The off-spring of purebred stock, assuming they are well taken care of during their growing age, are pretty apt to deviate little from their parents.

Another question that should be settled before you even start looking for your new family member is whether you want a male or female dog. Here I don't take sides. Through the years I have had just as much success training one as the other. There are more differences between various breeds than there are between the sexes, as far as smartness, loyalty, and wanderlust are concerned. Male and female puppies, treated and trained in the same manner, react in similar ways. I can't find any difference in their performances. Cost-wise you may find a bargain in the purchase of a female, because there is usually more demand for the little male puppies, and they are therefore likely to command a somewhat higher price than their little sisters.

The deciding factor, I believe, will probably be your willingness to put up with the twice yearly periods during which the female will be in heat. This lasts for about 21 days as a rule. Depending upon yourself, the dog, your home, your neighborhood, and possibly your pocketbook, these periods will be either downright annoying or can pass with a minimum of fuss and inconvenience.

If you are fastidious you may object to keeping the dog in the house during these days, even though with some dogs the nuisance is very minor. If there are many dogs in your neighborhood it can be quite a test of your good humor to be followed by all the male strays in the county whenever you take your pet for its daily exercise. It may even not be surprising to find them waiting on your doorstep when you take her out of the house in the morning. So I think that I should advise you to plan on leaving your female pet at a boarding kennel during these semi-annual periods. Before making your purchase of a little female puppy you might inquire what it will cost you to board her once or twice a year, if money is a factor in your family life.

Still another solution to owning a female dog is to have it spayed. De-sexing it makes it impossible for it to be bred, and when properly done it is not objectionable as far as the dog's health is concerned. Spaying may, or may not, cause the animal to grow fat and sluggish. You can get conflicting opinions on this matter from different sources, therefore I advise you to consult the veterinarian you would have do the job before you purchase a female puppy, if you intend to have this operation performed. The doctor will tell you what he thinks about it, and about its effect on the dog's health and temperament. He will also tell you at what age, in his opinion, your pup should have her operation.

The next consideration may not affect you. It won't if you have already made up your mind to buy a purebred animal, because that is the subject of this question. To buy a purebred or a mongrel? There is much to be said for the first choice and little for the other. The persistent myth that mongrels are smarter than purebreds is just not true. In many cases they are equally smart, it is true, but as for being in general brighter than their blue-blooded relatives — don't believe it.

A mongrel may be an appealing little baby dog, but by the time it is full grown it may be a living monstrosity — attractive only to its owner. There is no question but that many of the cross-bred dogs have good qualities, but they also are very apt to have various unknown ones too. Why take a chance? If its money that influences you, just reflect a moment. You pay the first cost but once, and you are buying a little friend that will likely be an intimate member of your family for many years. Once you have the pet you will find that the cost of maintaining a purebred is no higher than that of a mut. One eats as much as the other. Indeed, medical care is apt to be higher for the ordinary mongrel than for the purebred. The latter is more likely to have a heritage of good health and care.

There are still other factors which should be considered if you have much thought of acquiring a pet of little known ancestry. What about pride of ownership? Much as you might get to love a little nondescript animal it would be pretty hard to work up much pride in his appearance, in most cases. If you have a specific purpose in mind for your dog, other than being the family companion and pet, you will surely choose the breed that has shown the greatest adaptability along the lines you desire. In other words, if you would like to go into the hunting field for a week or so in the fall you will probably choose a purebred known for its hunting skill; if you have in mind a guardian as well as a pet you may be attracted to one of the well known guard dog breeds. In cases like these you surely won't let one of your main reasons for getting a dog be left to chance in its fulfillment.

If, however, you do acquire a pet of mixed parentage you should be sure to treat it just as well as you would a high priced pup from an expensive kennel. Don't neglect him just because he was easy to come by.

Under some conditions, size of the mature dog will have a definite bearing on your choice. If you live in the country, in a village, or on an estate with plenty of wide open space for the dog to exercise, size of the animal won't play much of a part in its selection. Or if you live in a house with enough ground around it to have

In picking your puppy choose one that is playful, aggressive, and healthy. The overly aggressive one can be controlled, but an exceedingly shy one may be a disappointment all his life.

a fenced run for the dog you will not be hampered much by size in your choice.

For those who live in the city, especially in an apartment, the size of a dog does have a direct bearing on the ease of maintaining him. Theoretically at least, the larger the dog the more exercise he needs. Thus, if you will find it inconvenient to take long walks once or twice every day, you may decide that a small dog will be better for you than a large one. Again, as a general rule, the larger the dog, the more he eats. If this means anything to you you should keep it in mind when making your selection. Size of the dog (the grown dog, that is) is important also if your rooms are small and heavily furnished with small breakables. More than once I have seen one swipe of a big friendly Great Dane's tail send a cup and saucer or other fragile piece clattering to the floor. I don't say that a small dog is a guarantee against all accidents and breakage but it is one more point to consider.

In favor of large dogs, however, is the fact that most of them are wonderfully gentle and quiet; in fact, the larger the dog the more dignified he is, in most cases. Just so that you won't think I am prejudiced in either direction I want to tell you that I have two house dogs, a very

small one, a Miniature Schnauzer, and a large Doberman. We love them both.

Don't pick out your future canine pal without being aware, at least, of the fact that dogs do shed their hair. Some people find this is annoying, especially when the condition persists over a long period of time instead of just for a short while as is normal. Daily grooming and proper feeding will in most cases make shedding of minor importance but it is well to know beforehand that it is a problem. For this reason many people choose a short-haired breed, as they do not have as much hair to shed nor is the hair quite as objectionable as the long hair dropped by some breeds. I would not let this fact have too much weight in choosing a dog for myself, though, because I know that just a little daily work will practically eliminate the problem. We'll cover this more thoroughly in the later chapter on grooming.

If you have one particular breed in mind when you actually start out to look for your new puppy you had better confine your shopping to this breed, because it's awfully easy to loose your heart to nearly any little pup. You are apt to see one of a type far removed from what you have decided that you want, and be completely taken in by his cute antics and friendly ways;

first thing you know you will have bought him. So I'm warning you to be definite in your search if one certain breed best fits your requirements.

There are several obvious places to search for your puppy. Attend the nearest dog show and look over the mature dogs of the breed in which you are interested. Talk to the exhibitors. Remember, if you are looking for a family pet instead of a potential show dog, you may get a bargain by taking a pup with an excellent pedigree but which is not a particularly good example of the breed. It may be just fine for a pet, but not quite good enough in conformation to show much possibility as a future show dog. But even so it may be a handsome animal, as the fine points it lacks may be discernable only to a professional.

Find out where the breeding kennels in your vicinity are and visit them. Very often you can find exactly what you want in this way; if not right at the moment of your visit most professional kennels have litters coming along at frequent intervals.

Good pet stores can often be of assistance in your search. Many sell pups at their stores, and others have connections with breeders of the various types of dogs. By dealing with a reputable store of this kind you can quickly find what pups are available in your chosen breed and price range. If you live in a large city there will be any number of pet shops within reasonable distance of your home or office. Get acquainted with one or more of them and tell them just what you are looking for.

Don't forget the dog and pet magazines. Their classified and display columns are full of ads offering dogs and puppies of all breeds and ages. Many of the breeders will ship a dog on approval, although if the advertiser is a consistent exhibitor you are pretty sure to get a pup fully meeting the description in the advertisement.

Unless you are an old hand at raising puppies you should not get one much less than ten or twelve weeks old. I mean you should not take one home if he is younger than this. It is certainly all right, and quite a common practice, to buy a pup younger than this but to leave him at the kennel with his mother until he is around three months old. The first two or three months of any pup's life should be spent with his mother.

Look your prospective purchase over very carefully. If possible take a dog-wise friend with you when you visit the kennel or pet shop. Don't buy if the dogs are not kept in a clean place, and if the surroundings do not indicate that the dogs are well cared for in all ways. Make sure, if you can, that the puppy isn't afflicted with rickets: he should have strong, sturdy, and straight front legs. His eyes should be clear and free from mucous; if he shows any signs of a cold be doubly careful. In fact, it is a splendid idea to insist that you get a veterinarian's OK before the sale becomes final.

I always like to pick a pup that is friendly and somewhat aggressive, one that will play without much urging and that does not cringe when approached. Get down on your knees and hold out your hands to him. Does he shy away, or does he wag his little tail and come to you? If he is excessively shy you are likely to have too much trouble training him. Other things being equal, pick the bold, playful little fellow.

Of course you must be gentle in your approach to any puppy. If you go dashing up to any little baby and startle it by your loud talk and rough actions you will scare the dickens out of it. Take your time in getting it to come to you, and talk quietly and gently as you let it look you over. Don't try to rush things too much.

Before you take the new member of your family home you should have a few things ready for it there, at least a place to sleep, food and drink, and a plan for housebreaking.

GETTING ACQUAINTED WITH YOUR NEW DOG

Take time in making friends with any strange dog. We always let a new dog take the initiative in getting acquainted. Caution your children that they should not try to pet strange dogs they pass on the streets. Never, never try to "corner" an unknown animal.

Transferring to a new home can be a fairly trying experience for a dog, especially for a little puppy unused to being away from its mother. It is important, therefore, for the new owner to make the transition as smooth as can be done.

Normally, your new pet will arrive at your house by one of two methods. You may call for him at his kennel or other home and carry him back with you, or he will be delivered to you by the seller or his agent, possibly the Express Company. In either case don't rush your wel-

come too much, don't overwhelm him at your meeting. Let him get accustomed to you by easy stages. In other words, introduce yourself to him in an easy, relaxed way. Too loud and brisk manners are apt to scare him half out of his wits.

If you have gone to the kennels or pet store to pick him up, spend a little time with him in his familiar surroundings before packing him up and removing him from all he has known up to this time. Play with him quietly for a few minutes if he seems interested. Talk calmly to

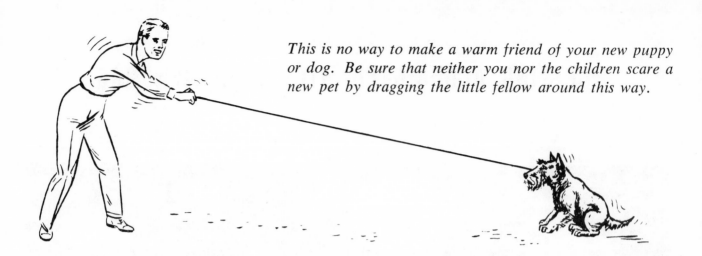

This is no way to make a warm friend of your new puppy or dog. Be sure that neither you nor the children scare a new pet by dragging the little fellow around this way.

the little fellow. Let him be the one to make the aggressive moves. Get down on your knees and hold out your hands invitingly, meantime encouraging his approach by soft quiet words. Don't rush him; let him take his time.

Above all, don't back a dog into a corner and then try to pick him up. This may well terrify a puppy, and frighten a grown dog to the point of growling or biting. In making friends with a strange animal it is always advisable to let it take the initiative. As a rule, as soon as it satisfies itself that you are friendly, and mean it no harm, it will accept you and lose any fear of you it might otherwise have.

After reasonably friendly relations have thus been established you can get ready to take him home with you.

If your new pet is a young puppy, unused to car riding, not yet housebroken, it will be wise to put it in a basket or some kind of a container for the ride to your home. Its immaturity, the excitement, and the motion of the car can have disastrous results unless you are well prepared for all possible trouble. (If accidents of any kind do befall the pup on the first trip, be sure to keep calm — don't blame the little fellow because he'll be feeling much worse than you will in any case.)

If instead of picking up the new dog yourself, you have had him delivered right to your house, you still should make an effort to introduce yourself to the new arrival in a manner calculated to put him at his ease. If it is an older dog, or a housebroken puppy, let him have the run of the place for a while, looking things over at his leisure, and at the same time sizing you up. If the new pet is a pup, and not yet housebroken, it will be best to put him in a small room with an easily cleaned floor (not carpeted) and let him wander about by himself for a while.

I wouldn't feed a dog immediately, while he is still excited and probably a little nervous. A dish of water, though, should be offered, because he will no doubt be thirsty. Just set it on the floor in whatever location you are going to reserve for his eating and drinking area. Let him find it by himself, and drink if he feels like doing so.

If you have young children in the family it is going to be a little hard to keep them separated from the dog at this time, but it is something you should do. Oh, it's all right to let them sit down on the floor and let the pup sniff around them and be petted a little. But no rough play, and very little, if any, handling. Left to his own devices, a little puppy will want to take a nap soon after his first hour or so in his new home.

And this brings us to preparations which you should make before bringing the pet home, preparations for its sleeping comfort, dishes for food and water as well as food itself, and a collar and leash to be used when it is taken out for exercise. The next chapter will suggest convenient and comfortable arrangements for the dog's bed and bedding.

SLEEPING ARRANGEMENTS FOR YOUR DOG

The first decision to be made regarding the dog's sleeping quarters is the one of whether he will sleep in the house or out of doors. Of course this is not a question if you live in an apartment for in such case the dog will for sure sleep indoors. But where space outdoors permits, some owners provide an outside kennel for their pet dog.

Indoors, the main requirement is that the dog have a suitable bed, placed in a spot out of the way of the regular family traffic through the rooms, and removed from drafts and all extremes of temperature.

The bed itself can be very simple. A cushion, if thick enough to be comfortable, will serve all right, unless your floor is cold or damp. In this case a cushion should be held up off the floor by some sort of rack or frame. The main thing, in fixing a bed, is to make sure that it is draft free. Some locations in some rooms would require protective sides on the bed to shield the pet from breezes.

If you are fixing just a temporary bed, to take care of the pup for but a short time, you might get a box from one of the stores in the neighborhood. Furnish this with an old cushion, or a plentiful supply of scraps of old clothes. Be sure it is large enough that the puppy can get in and out easily, as well as stretch out and have plenty of space to rest and sleep easily. Be certain that it is not placed where it will be in the way of the family members as they pass through the room. If the puppy is not housebroken you will be wise to rig up some kind of a little fence around his bed and play area. It won't take up much space and can be quite effective in this part of the dog's training. Put a few thicknesses of newspaper in one corner of the enclosure.

If you are buying a permanent bed for the dog you will find a large choice of sizes and types at any good pet supply store. You will find dog beds made of wicker, wood, and metal. A variety of colors are also offered. In addition to regular beds there are thick cushions, some having raised backs and sides around them. The one caution to keep in mind is that the bed should be large enough to allow full relaxed stretching out by the dog. Get the advice of an expert on the size to buy, especially if your dog is not full-grown and you are not sure how big he is likely to be when he has attained his full stature.

Sturdy construction and ample size are necessary if the dog's bed is to be used for training as well as sleeping quarters for your pet.

If you have a corner of the room which you can turn over to the exclusive use of the dog so much the better. Such a spot will give the dog a feeling of proprietorship; dogs as well as humans need a place to which they can retreat and be undisturbed every so often. When the puppy feels that everything is wrong and everyone is against him, he'll carry one or two of his playthings to his corner and lie in his bed meditating on what a tough world this is. Soon as he gets up, though, he'll be right back in the thick of family life, ready for more play as usual.

If you have room outside for a kennel you may be interested in providing one for your pet. The size of such a house should vary as the size of your dog, of course, but be sure it is large enough so that your animal will have plenty of room. In addition to the kennel itself there must be a runway, fenced, unless you live in the country and feel perfectly safe in allowing the dog to run free. Even with plenty of space, however, I am against allowing any dog to roam at will, at least until he has had a thorough course in obedience training and will not leave the premises. Letting a puppy run around the neighborhood is an excellent way to spoil him forever. He's apt to start chasing cars, other dogs, visiting your friends and begging food,

and in general making a nuisance of himself.

So my advice to you is to keep your pup under control at all times. This means that you fence him in if he sleeps outdoors. Make his run out of cinders or gravel if possible. And make it long and narrow rather than square. This encourages him to get more exercise; he'll run from one end to the other.

The kennel structure itself should be wind and waterproof, and if you live in one of the cold winter climates it should be adequately insulated. One more requisite is that it should be built in such a way that the roof can be opened up to the air and sunlight. Absolute cleanliness is essential. Dry, clean straw makes a good bedding material, or you can make a mattress out of ticking and fill it with bits of shredded foam rubber or fibreglass.

One idea to keep in mind when building or buying a kennel is that dogs like a flat or gently sloping roof. They like to get up on such a roof and lie in the sun, especially when the weather has been bad and the ground is wet or damp.

Indoors or out, give your dog a good place to rest and sleep. After all, don't forget that they spend many hours a day with little else to do, so make it as pleasant and comfortable for them as you can.

PROPER FEEDING IS VERY IMPORTANT

A book on training does not allow much space for the subject of feeding the dog. The subject is so important, however, that at least the general principles of proper food must be touched upon. A well fed dog is receptive to training lessons — at least it isn't hungry, weak, or sluggish all of the time.

It may be somewhat of a surprise to you, but it is a fact that dogs thrive on about the same kind of a diet that humans need, with the exception that dogs do not seem to need vitamin C. Dogs need flesh and tissue building proteins, energy and heat producing fats, carbohydrates which supply energy, bone building minerals, and various vitamins, necessary for a great many purposes. Tests over many years, and by a large number of competent scientists, have proven beyond a doubt that all of these components are necessary to the good health of the dog.

Poor feeding, which means providing food which is seriously lacking in any of the basic requirements, has been proven to be the cause of many if not most of the ailments to which canines are subject. Skin troubles, such as constant scratching and serious loss of hair in spots, lack of pep and energy, diarrhea, nervousness, poor condition of coat, and many others have been traced directly in many cases to poor nutrition.

This being so, how are you going to feed your dog? There are several ways it *can* be done correctly. You can buy a good book on the subject of dog nutrition, study it, keep a supply of the necessary raw materials in the house and cook and feed them to your pet as directed. That's one way, but a tough way, I think. Another way is to feed scraps from your table, being careful to see that the dog gets as balanced a diet each day as your family does. This, of course, was the way all dogs were fed years ago, except that their owners did not give any thought at all to the proper ingredients of the pet's daily fare. One day he might have all meat, or for several days running, and other times it might run practically all to fats or carbohydrates. No thought at all was given to vitamins or minerals.

This hit or miss feeding wasn't too bad in some cases because most dogs were allowed to run about the neighborhood and they made up, via begging at the back doors and raiding the garbage cans, some of the deficiencies. But now, in cities especially, and always with knowing owners, dogs are kept home, where they should be. They are thus entirely dependent on what their master gives them.

The third way, and by far the best, is to serve them high grade commercial dog food, a canned meat or a dry meat-cereal food, or a combination of both. But pick a good one. Just as with most things offered for sale there are good dog foods and poor ones, some very poor. I can't tell you here the ones that I have found to be good. Ask your vet for his advice, or choose one of the labels that you know, from your own experience, stands for high quality in all food products they put out.

As for amounts to feed and frequencies and times to give the food, you should consult your vet or the kennel owner from whom you bought your puppy. Either one will be able and willing to give you trustworthy advice.

A high-protein canned or frozen meat food. The favorite of many.

The kibble type of dry food — high in nourishment and flavor.

A dry meal type of food requires only the addition of water.

High-protein biscuits are made in many shapes and sizes.

You can make it easy, and safe, to feed your dog. High grade commercial dog foods contain all of the ingredients necessary to nourish a dog perfectly.

Puppies, just as human babies, need to be fed small amounts often, at least five times a day when they are no more than two months old. As they grow older the frequency is lessened; from two to four months they will probably need four feedings per day; between four and six months the meals can be dropped to three daily; from then until they reach their first birthday two times a day will be enough.

When a dog reaches the age of twelve months he can safely be fed but once a day, and this should generally be in the late afternoon. Some owners supplement this daily "big" meal with a light breakfast for their pets, maybe a handful of kibbles with a little milk.

I want to caution you about several points

having to do with the proper feeding habits, both from the standpoint of the health of the puppy and the pleasure you should normally get from owning and keeping a pet in your home. The following advice is given with the definite knowledge that it works; if you will follow it you will have the best chance to raise a healthy, well behaved, obedient dog.

FEEDING TIPS

1. Give your dog his own dishes, one for food and one for water.
2. Keep the dishes scrupulously clean.
3. Feed the dog in the same place every day, in a place where he can eat without being disturbed.
4. Feed him at the same time every day.
5. Regulate his food carefully. By this I mean that you should gage the amount he needs by his condition. If he tends to gain too much weight on his daily ration you should cut down on it a little. If he becomes too thin, add to it somewhat.
6. After the dog has had a reasonable length of time in which to eat his food, take up the dish and do not offer him more until his next regular feeding time. Do not leave a dish of half-eaten food in front of the dog for long.
7. Never feed the dog between his regular meals. This means that he will not be fed tidbits from your dining table.
8. Do not allow him to roam the neighborhood in search of food (or for any other reason).
9. Never allow the dog to be teased while he is eating.
10. See that he has access to fresh clean water at all times.
11. Remember that the dog will need more food when he is active than when he has but little exercise.
12. Dogs really do not need, nor expect, variety in their diets. They can and do relish a good nourishing food day after day. Special, though tasty, treats are apt to make them finicky eaters. If you know that you are giving your pet a good all-inclusive food you can safely serve it to him day in and day out; he'll enjoy it and thrive on it, and you will not have the unpleasant task of coaxing him to eat.
13. It won't be anything to worry about if your dog's appetite varies a little. I'm sure that your own isn't the same every day; sometimes you are really hungry and sometimes you have little interest in food. But if coupled with no appetite the dog actually acts sick, if he has a "runny" nose, seems to want to hide away by himself, or otherwise doesn't act "right," you have reasons to suspect that he might need the vet's attention. Several dog maladies start with such symptoms. So be watchful if food is refused for more than one meal.

If you observe the above rules you should have no trouble with your pet's food, and if he is thus properly fed he is unlikely to be on the sick list, in the ordinary course of events.

DOGS SHOULD BE WELL GROOMED

All dogs should be kept clean; for house dogs, of course, cleanliness is an absolute necessity. It takes but a few moments each day to keep a dog's coat and skin in good shape, mainly by vigorous brushing. In addition to keeping the coat in tiptop condition, you should regularly inspect and care for the animal's feet, teeth, nails, nose, ears and eyes. All this is not as burdensome as it sounds.

The easiest and probably the best way to conduct this chore (unless you have an outsize dog) is to put the animal up on a table or box. Grooming the dog when he is on a table or other raised platform makes it easy on you — eliminates a lot of stooping and bending. It has an even more important advantage, though, in that it makes a dog much more amenable to your attentions than he would be if he were left on the ground; the slight feeling of insecurity the dog suffers tends to keep him quiet.

Provide yourself with a brush and comb of the proper type for your dog's coat. The comb won't be used very much as you will need it only to untangle the snarls which won't come out by brushing. (If you have a short-coated dog you won't need a comb at all.) Rub the hair and skin of the dog very briskly with your finger tips — this will loosen any dead hair. Then brush it thoroughly, first against the direction the hair lies, then with. Regular treatment of this kind will do a great deal to give your dog a very handsome coat, in addition to keeping it free from objectionable odors and parasites. A valuable plus is that hairs which would ordinarily be shed upon carpets, furniture and clothes, will be taken out by the brush. Housewives are quick to appreciate this.

Many owners never bathe their dogs. Dogs do not perspire through their skin, and, because of this, bathing is unnecessary except in instances in which the coat becomes soiled from outside sources. Ordinary dust and dirt will be easily removed by the daily brushing. One argument against bathing a dog frequently is that it removes oils from the coat, tending to make it dry, rough, and brittle.

For those times when a bath is really necessary you may buy preparations especially compounded for this purpose. All pet supply stores carry dog shampoos, both the "dry cleaners" and regular soaps or detergents to be used with water. If you use dry bath preparations all you have to do is to follow directions, being careful to keep the material out of the pet's eyes, ears, and nose.

To give the dog a good old-fashioned bath there are a few precautions you should make. First, the water must not be too hot. About 105 degrees is right. Next, in order to be sure that soap does not get into the pet's eyes, squeeze a small amount of yellow oxide of mercury or a drop of castor oil into each. Then, to protect the inner canals of the ears, put balls of cotton in the outer ears. (Don't push this far into the ears; just fill up the outer openings, so that it can be easily removed after the bath.)

After soaping and rubbing the dog's coat well be sure to rinse all of the shampoo out of it. Several changes of water are necessary for this, or, better yet, use running water through a spray nozzle.

Always dry the dog thoroughly, using enough dry towels. If it is in the summer, and warm and sunny, let him romp around for awhile after his towelling, but if the weather is damp or cold it is better to keep him indoors until he is dry enough that there is no danger of catching cold.

If you want to clip, pluck or trim your dog according to the approved standard for its breed you should buy a grooming chart at your pet supply dealer. These are available for most all of the breeds, and are inexpensive and very helpful. In addition you might watch an expert fix up your dog or another of the same kind. There's quite a trick to getting some dogs done up just right!

EYES

There isn't much that you can or should do about your dog's eyes, other than to be quick to notice any unnatural condition that may develop. When a dog is in good health his eyes will, as a general rule, mirror such a condition. Conversely, many diseases, especially virus ailments, signal their onset by disturbance of the eyes. Be sure to present your pet to the vet immediately if there should be a mucous discharge from its eyes. In addition, any time they do not look just right, while at the same time the dog doesn't act as usual, you should be on the alert for further symptoms. Do not let such conditions persist for long before getting professional advice.

Some owners bathe their dog's eyes, once or twice a week, with a lukewarm solution of boric acid. This is a good idea but eyes are such delicate organs that extensive "home" remedies and doctoring should not be attempted, except under explicit orders of your veterinarian.

EARS

Dogs with long ear flaps often are troubled by accumulations of sticky, thick wax in the inner ear canals. The ear flaps were designed by nature to act as shields against the entrance of foreign matter into the ears. They serve well for this purpose, but some dogs have been bred to have such long and heavy flaps that not enough air to ventilate the inner canal gets past them.

This wax must be removed frequently enough to prevent it from becoming troublesome. Inspect the ears once or twice a week, and when wax is visible make a swab of cotton, dip this into a solution of boric acid, and gently swab out the wax. *Do not* probe into the inner canal, and be very gentle and careful throughout this procedure. Use as many swabs as are necessary in order to remove all the visible wax.

Poodles, retrievers and spaniels are most susceptible to this trouble. Excessive growth of hair inside the ears can also be troublesome, and when you note such a condition you should clip it away, before it becomes matted and tangled.

Examine your dog's teeth occasionally to make sure that they are in good shape, clean and sound.

If you notice your dog twitching his ears, shaking its head, and constantly trying to scratch its ears, you should take pity on it and hustle it to its vet for his expert attention.

Simple cleaning of the dog's ears should be a daily routine with you. Brushing gently, and cleaning away all traces of dirt and food particles will generally suffice.

TEETH

Yes, dogs have dental problems too! Trouble can range from deposits of tartar (which should be removed) to decayed, worn, loosened, or abscessed teeth. While a dog can be subject to any of these dental troubles (as well as others) it is not uncommon for a dog to have clean, sound teeth all his life. Sensible care on the owner's part has a lot to do with it.

It is an easy job to keep your dog's teeth free from tartar deposits. All that is necessary is an occasional cleaning with a stiff toothbrush and an approved dentrifrice, or a mixture of household salt, bicarbonate of soda, and pumice powder.

If the tartar is so thick and heavy that it effectively resists brushing, you should have it removed by the veterinarian, and then in the future be careful not to let it accumulate again.

Meat bones are not a necessary part of the dog's diet. It is certainly true that they like them, and adult dogs can digest them, but constant gnawing on bones will wear down the teeth dangerously. Then, when the enamel is worn off, it is easy for decay to complete the ruin. Further, even if the teeth are not harmed by the bones, chewing them entails other dangers. Some bones are very brittle, and when these (as well as tiny ones) are swallowed, they may injure, by puncturing or scraping, the stomach or intestines. All in all, feeding bones to your dog is bad business — you have nothing to gain but much to lose.

NAILS

Many owners neglect the important task of caring for their dog's nails. The nails grow quite fast and should be examined every six months or oftener. If they are allowed to become too long they may break, or they may turn upward and into the pads of the feet. Another danger of too long nails is that sometimes they get caught on something and are ripped right out of the flesh. As you can imagine, this is very painful to the animal.

Before attempting to cut or file them yourself for the first time you should have your veterinarian show you how the job is done and how long they should be allowed to grow. After instruction you will find that the job is easy to do with a rasp or clippers which are available at all dog supply stores.

Dew claws are the ones which grow high on a dog's feet — they correspond to our thumbs and big toes. They do not reach the ground at all, serve no purpose, and are not worn off by contact with the ground. It is therefore recommended that they be surgically removed by the vet, thus doing away with any possibility that they will be caught and torn. If you live where your dog is active in the fields and woods, or if the family pet on occasion doubles as a hunting companion, you will be wise to have these dew claws removed before they are torn off on a fence or rough brush in the field.

NOSE

The only time a dog's nose needs your attention is when it incurs an injury, such as a deep scratch or cut. Then, unless the harm is severe, it is usually enough to see that it is kept clean.

A dry nose, or an excessively wet nose, may indicate that all is not well with the dog's health, but on the whole this is not a reliable indication of anything. More often than not such signs should be ignored. A *continuing* discharge from the nose does mean that there is a real danger present, however, and the dog should be taken to his doctor post haste. The dreaded distemper is but one disease that heralds its approach in this manner.

ANAL GLANDS

The anal glands are small glands located on the sides of a dog's rectum. Sometimes these become impacted, causing severe discomfort and pain to the animal. When the dog scrubs along the floor or ground on his posterior he is trying to relieve this situation. It is kindness to take him to his vet and have the glands cleared.

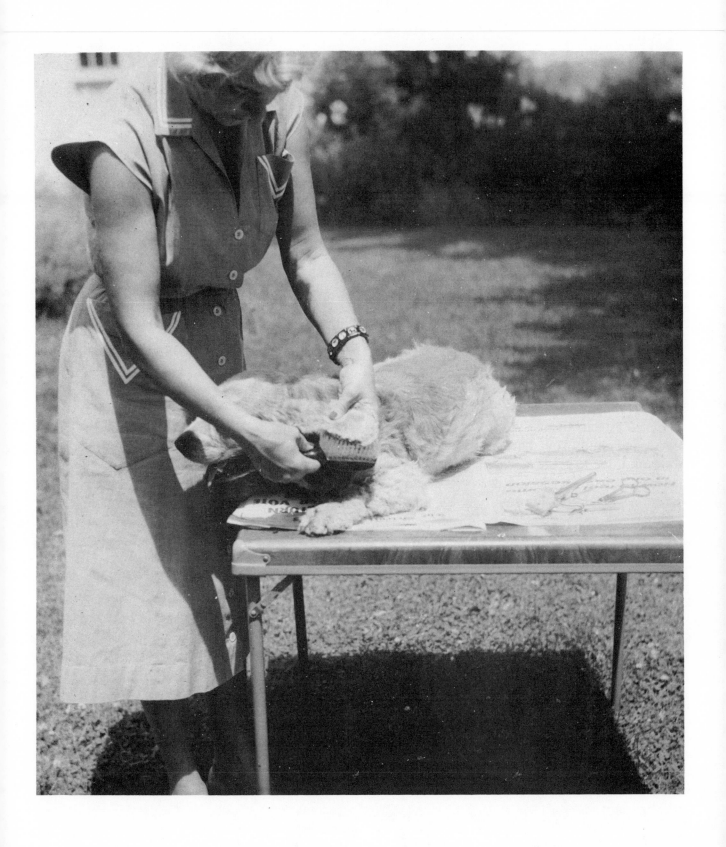

A card table makes a good grooming stand for most dogs. Unless it's an old one it should be protected from scratches from the dog's nails.

If this happens often you may ask the doctor to show you the treatment (it is simple) so that you can take care of it yourself in the future.

Skin Parasites

Fleas, lice, and ticks are parasites which attach themselves to dogs at every opportunity. All of them are obnoxious, even dangerous, if allowed to remain on the animal. Fortunately, it is easy to control them by using the modern preparations which have been developed for this purpose.

Fleas are the most common. There are liquids and powders obtainable at any pet supply counter which are easily applied and very effective in the removal of these pests. Some are to be sprayed on the animal, some put into a solution into which the dog will be dipped, and others are in a powder form to be dusted on and into the dog's coat. Take your choice!

Fleas attach themselves to a dog easily. Grass and sandy soils harbor them while they wait for a dog to come along and pick them up. An unfortunate fact is that flea eggs do not remain on the dog but drop off onto the animal's bedding, where they hatch and spend the early part of their lives. Because of this it is necessary to disinfect the bedding very thoroughly if your pet has had fleas on him.

Lice fasten themselves directly to the dog's body, biting and sucking the skin. Both fleas and lice act as hosts to the canine tapeworm, perpetuating a vicious circle. To find lice, if the dog is afflicted with them, use a strong light, and search the skin carefully. The face, neck, and shoulders of a dog are favorite spots of the louse.

You can have your veterinarian remove them from your dog or you can do this job yourself. Make a solution of water-base 2% DDT, or use one of the ready-made preparations which pet shops sell. They are easy to use when directions are followed.

There are many types of ticks but only two of them are commonly found on dogs. One is the Wood-tick and the other is the Brown-tick. The former lives in open fields, the latter is found indoors, in kennels, barns, and even in homes. Extreme care should be taken in dealing with these parasites, as some are carriers of a disease which is dangerous to humans as well as dogs.

Some parts of the country are heavily infested with ticks while others have few or none. You are lucky if your locality is free from them. If you live where ticks thrive you should look your dog over often, at least once a day if he spends any time in the grass. Ticks bury their heads in the skin of the dog, and if left in this position they swell up to many times their normal size through sucking the dog's blood. When you find one attached to your pet take care in removing it. Do not try to pull it directly from the skin. The best way is to put a small amount of ether on a piece of cotton and hold this on the tick for a moment, after which it is easy to pull him away. Use a pair of tweezers for this purpose, and finish it by dropping the pest into a fire or a bottle of alcohol which you should keep for this use. Lacking ether, put the lighted end of a cigarette against the tick before removing it.

If your dog becomes loaded with the creatures bathe him in a solution of DDT, a 4% mixture, water-based. Also disinfect his bedding with this same kind of disinfectant.

HOW TO HOUSEBREAK YOUR PUPPY QUICKLY

Housebreaking is a bugaboo that scares some people from buying a puppy. I'll admit that it may be the least enjoyable part of owning a dog, but when you stack up the inconvenience of two or three weeks of training against ten or fifteen years of pleasure with a dog, the period of housebreaking seems unimportant after all.

I am often asked questions about housebreaking dogs, and two of the most frequently put questions are (1) How long should it take to train a puppy and (2) Can all puppies be successfully housebroken? My answers sometimes seem unsatisfactory to the questioners because they are not rigidly definite. In answer to the first question I know that the length of time depends as much upon the trainer as upon the dog. If the person is as faithful in his training duties as he expects his pup to be, the job can sometimes be accomplished in a week or ten days. If the person is slipshod in his training the dog might still be untrained many weeks later. It is entirely *possible* (and easy) to housebreak a dog in a fairly short time!

The answer to the second question, in my opinion, is a qualified yes. This does not mean that all learn in the same length of time, because there is quite a difference in the mentality of different dogs. Some learn quickly, some very slowly. I have seen some dogs that were never reliable in the house, but even these knew better, I am sure. I repeat that all dogs can be housebroken, but even so, some, through perverseness, spite, or laziness, can never be completely trusted. Fortunately, these dogs are greatly in the minority. For all practical purposes you can safely assume that your puppy can be easily trained in this matter.

The mechanics of housebreaking a puppy are very simple. You merely take advantage of two facts of dog behavior. The first is that dogs, even puppies, are inherently clean animals. The second is that pups do have to go, often, and at fairly predictable times.

In training you may utilize the first fact by closely confining the little fellow until he has learned his lessons. Keep him in a small area, close to his bed. Tie him with a small, lightweight chain, or let him be free but fenced into a small space right near his bed. If this is done he will quickly come to the point where he will resist soiling his quarters except when he can't help it.

The second, and most important part of the training, consists of giving the animal every opportunity to relieve himself at the approved place, either outdoors or on papers. If you live in an apartment house, or it is wintertime, you may elect to train the pup to paper, in which case you put him on folded newspapers at the proper times. Later, when he is partially trained, you take up the papers and send him outside.

At first it will require many trips to the papers or the outdoors. In general, give him a chance following each of three activities: eating, sleeping, playing. Within a few moments of the time he finishes eating or drinking hustle the pup outdoors and keep him there until he performs. As soon as he wakes up, whether from his night sleep or one of his frequent daytime naps, take him out. After a session of romping and playing see that he goes out before he makes a mistake in the house. In between these times watch him carefully, unless he is in his pen, and rush him to the proper

The magic times to take your puppy out!
After eating — after playing — after sleeping.

place whenever he starts sniffing nervously along the floor.

Follow these procedures and you will find that your pet will soon know what is expected of him and will try hard to cooperate.

When he does make a mistake in the house don't let it upset you to the point of being harsh with the little pup. Scold him, shame him, take him outside. If a mistake was made long before you discover it it won't do you a bit of good, though, to punish him in any way. You'll only confuse him. Unless you catch him at the time he won't know what it is that he did wrong. Don't lose sight of the fact that a puppy is just a baby — show him all the consideration that you can.

No matter how young your pup is I wouldn't feed him later than five P. M. nor give him drinking water any later in the day than three hours before his last outing before bedtime.

Never neglect to take him out when he should go, no matter what the weather nor what other things you would rather do. To fail in your duty is inexcusable, and puts off for a long time the day when you can call the dog really housebroken.

Whenever you do take him out you should find as secluded a spot for him as possible, away from distracting sights and noises, so that the little fellow won't forget what he is out there for. And when you do find a spot that the puppy will use you should take him back there each time, if possible. The suggestion this gives him will shorten the time you will have to stay out.

Be sure that your puppy does not have worms, because if he does it will greatly complicate your job of housebreaking him.

Praise the dog lavishly each time he does as he should.

TRAVEL TIPS FOR MOTORING PLEASURE

Train your dog to ride quietly, in either the front or the back seat. It can be very dangerous to have a dog jumping around the interior of a car in motion.

Most family dogs are required to do a certain amount of traveling with the members of the household. This may range from regular trips to the nearest shopping center up to long distance jaunts involving days at a time. If you prepare your dog for traveling, these trips can be very pleasant, but with an unruly, sick or nervous pet in the car, they can be anything but pleasurable. So take a little time at the beginning and teach your dog good traveling manners.

Most dogs like to ride in an automobile, but some are nervous and scared at first. Both the motion and the sound seem to bother them, so it is well to introduce them to the experience with care.

Put the collar and leash on the dog. Use some command to tell the animal to get into the car. "Up" is all right. You will have to exert a little pressure on the leash to get him in, no doubt, but don't scare him. When he makes it have him sit on a seat, not on anyone's lap. Do not allow him to put his paws on a window sill nor poke his head out a window. If you are going to do the driving on this first ride for the pup you should have a companion to keep the dog under control in the seat.

Start the motor, and if he seems to accept the sound without much fuss you can start off. Before the lesson starts be sure that you allow the dog exercise, and you should refrain from giving him water for some time before.

Once the ride starts you must be on the watch for the animal to show signs of motion sickness. If the saliva begins to flow from his lips and tongue and if he trembles unduly you must slow down. If the signs continue it will be well to stop entirely. Take the dog out of the car and let him walk around a few minutes. When he seems to have returned to normal repeat the procedure of getting in and resuming the ride. You may have to stop quite a few times but this is better to do than to have him be sick in the car. One or two short trips will likely suffice to get him so accustomed to riding that he will look forward to each experience.

If you are going on long trips where your dog might be unwelcome don't forget that all cities have a few boarding kennels where dogs may be left at moderate charges. Very often this is the best plan and offers the least inconvenience to all, including the dog.

Another way of transporting a dog long distances without discomfort to the family or dog is by air. Most airlines have light shipping crates for this purpose and take good care of the pets during the trips, feeding and watering them as necessary.

A handy pamphlet to consult when planning a motor trip with a dog is the one put out by Gaines Kennels called "Traveling With Towser." This gives a list of the hotels and motels which welcome travelers with dogs. It is especially useful when you are following routes which are strange to you.

Don't forget, when planning on entering Canada with a dog, that the animal must have been vaccinated, and that you must have the proof with you.

TRAVEL TIPS

1. Do not allow your dog to ride with his head out a car window. This often results in injured eyes, as it is easy for foreign matter to enter them when he has his head in the air stream.

2. Feed the dog lightly before a long automobile trip. Just a small amount of water or milk, too.

3. Train the dog to sit quietly. It is dangerous to have a dog jumping around in a moving automobile.

4. On long trips carry the dog's feed and water dishes and be sure to offer him a drink whenever you stop to service your car.

5. Never leave your dog in a tightly closed car in the hot weather. Dogs have died from the effects of being imprisoned in the stiffling hot interiors of cars parked in the hot sun rays. If you must leave your pet in the car be sure to leave the windows down a little on each side, and park in shade if possible.

HOW TO KEEP YOUR DOG HEALTHY

Most dogs are rugged and need little medical attention. Good food is most important in keeping them well. Closely following this requirement might be listed, especially in the early years of the dog, proper inoculations against communicable diseases. Adequate sleeping arrangements, such as dry and clean bedding, freedom from extremes of heat and cold in the location of the bed, also rate high on the prevention list. Also, owners who keep their pets from roaming the neighborhood, picking up dirty or rancid food, and away from stray animals, have the best chance of keeping them in tip-top condition. Take care of your dog as you would any member of your family, but don't pamper or spoil it, and, barring accidents, you won't be likely to have much trouble.

When you first get the dog take it to the vet and have it examined for possible danger signs. If it has not had the necessary preventive shots, make arrangements at this time for them. It is most important that the dog be immunized against distemper at the proper time. Also against rabies. Your veterinarian will tell you the whole story on this score.

I am a great believer in early diagnosis of an ailment. If one of my dogs shows signs of illness I want the vet to look at him right away. I have found, over the years, that I have little trouble from serious illnesses in my kennels, proving to my satisfaction that this policy is cheap in the long run. There are a number of danger signs by which you can sometimes recognize the onslaught of a malady in your dog. If you notice one or more of these signals you will be wise to observe your dog very closely, and if the symptoms persist or new ones appear, get him to his veterinarian without further ado.

Different diseases have different symptoms, and it takes an expert to pin the correct label on each trouble. But there are certain departures from the normal dog behavior that are fairly easy to spot, and if these are detected in time and brought to the attention of a veterinarian the chances of a quick cure are good.

DANGER SIGNALS

1. Loss or slackening of normal appetite.

2. A rise in body temperature. (The normal temperature of a dog at rest is 101 degrees F. but it may vary as much as a full degree either way without being a cause for alarm. The temperature may be taken with a standard clinical thermometer via the dog's rectum. Moisten or oil the thermometer after it has been shaken down to 96 degrees, insert it and allow it to remain for about three minutes.)

3. Fast breathing, as noted by the rise and fall of the animal's flanks. This is not, however, very reliable in hot weather, as at this time the dog normally breathes quite fast.

4. Listlessness. You are the best judge of the normal behavior of your dog.

5. Droopy appearance. This too must be judged against his normal appearance.

6. Mucous discharge from eyes or nose.

7. Diarrhea or constipation.

8. Poor coat. Hair stands on end instead of lying flat against the body as it should. Also, skin should be "free" and should roll between your fingers easily. The coat should not be dull nor coarse, in either feel or appearance.

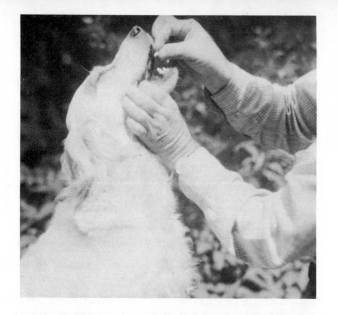

Pictures at left show how to give capsules or pills to a dog. Open his mouth wide and put the medicine far back on his tongue, then put your fingers around his jaws and hold his mouth shut for five or ten seconds.

For liquids the dose should be put in a small vial. Hold the dog's mouth closed, insert the end of the vial in the back part of his lips until the liquid drains down his throat.

INJURIES

There are many injuries to dogs which require first aid; cuts, broken bones, and burns may, if serious, require prompt action on the owner's part. If your dog is injured seriously try to get him to the vet's office with as little loss of time as possible.

Be very cautious in the way you handle an injured animal. Sometimes they are frantic with pain and will bite at anything, not knowing what they are doing. No matter what your pet's disposition may be in normal moments, no matter how well you think you know his every mood, do not give him the chance to bite you if and when he is injured. A seriously hurt dog

should be kept warm to avoid the danger of shock. If possible he should be taken to a veterinarian's office at once. If he can't be moved right away he should be covered by a blanket or a coat. If he is conscious put the blanket or coat over his head as you attempt to pick him up; this prevents him from biting you.

To sum up my advice on keeping your dog healthy, I say that if you feed him well, keep him clean, give him a clean, dry place to sleep, and do not allow him to roam, you stand a good chance of keeping him free from disease. If, in spite of good care, he does become ill, don't try to bring him through it without the expert help and advice of a veterinarian.

TRAINING EQUIPMENT

The articles which are necessary for training your dog are inexpensive, few in number, and readily available. All good pet supply sources carry everything that you will want.

You don't have to buy top quality for training purposes, of course, but you should make sure that whatever you use is strong enough for the job. This caution applies mostly to work with the big strong dogs, but even with the little fellows you will want leashes and collars that won't break easily.

You won't need everything at the start of the activities, but two items which must be on hand from the beginning are a short leash and an ordinary leather collar. These are necessary for even an untrained dog, so the list of special training items is really very short.

1. A short leash, five or six feet long, more or less, depending upon your own height. This may be made of any suitable material, leather, cotton webbing, plastic, or, of course, plain rope. Just be sure that it is strong enough to hold the animal for which it is intended.

2. One choke collar. This should be a welded chain collar, large enough so that when it is around the dog's neck there is still plenty of room for your hand to go between the collar and the animal's neck without squeezing.

3. Another leash, this one from 25 to 35 feet long. This may be of any lightweight but strong material. A common type is made of cotton webbing.

4. A strong ordinary leather collar. (I never use a harness on any dog.)

5. A tie-out stake and chain.

The above list covers all equipment needed for basic dog training. There are several other articles which can be used to good advantage, but are not strictly necessary.

1. A dumb-bell, if you plan to teach your pet to retrieve.

2. A Dog Anchor, available at many pet supply counters. This is a heavy suction cup attached to the end of a short length of chain. This will hold the dog when pressed firmly to a smooth, clean surface. Useful in teaching the dog to stay near his bed, near his housebreaking papers, or in keeping to his place in a car.

3. A dog mattress or a low box. In teaching a dog to STAY in one place I find it shortens the learning period if the dog is made to STAY on some sort of raised platform. The mattress or a low box serves well for this purpose.

4. A few dog toys. If the dog has his own toys, either homemade or bought especially for the purpose, there will be no excuse for him to play with, and chew up, good shoes and other household articles.

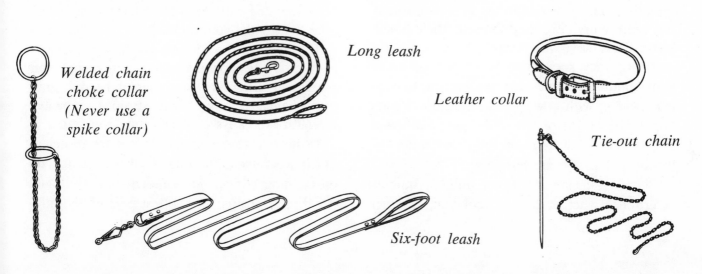

Welded chain choke collar (Never use a spike collar)

Long leash

Leather collar

Tie-out chain

Six-foot leash

GENERAL TRAINING PRINCIPLES

It is a lot of fun to train a dog. It's work, too, but the real sense of accomplishment that you earn by it is well worth it. It is true that a dog may endear itself to its master even though untrained and completely irresponsible, but ownership of a well-trained pet increases the pleasure many fold.

There is no mystery involved in teaching the average dog to behave, but, improperly taught, even a very fine dog can be ruined. There are certain basic principles of training which you should know and follow.

Do not attempt to train a puppy before it is old enough to absorb the lessons. (Housebreaking is an exception; it should be started as soon as the pup is brought into the home.) The best and quickest results, I believe, are obtained when a dog is trained when he is between the ages of one and four. Of course both older and younger dogs can be well trained. After a puppy has acquired his permanent teeth, is physically strong, and has dropped most of his baby ways, he is ready for serious training.

Right at the beginning you must establish yourself as the dog's master. This is very important! Either you or the dog will always have the dominant hand — one of you will "run" the other. This is not as funny as it may sound. I've seen many dogs that "bossed" their households. They were little tyrants. Spoiled and demanding, they knew that they could get away with minding no one. Do not confuse mastering the dog with cowing him. You don't want him to be afraid of you. You just want your dog to know that he must obey your orders — to know that you are his boss.

The dog, as an intelligent animal, quickly determines whether he can fool you, whether you are afraid of him, and whether you like him. To master him it's up to you to make him realize that you can't be fooled by him, that you are not the least bit afraid of him, and that while you do like him you don't intend to let him presume upon that fact. You must *demand* obedience, not just want it.

There are two ways to give commands to your dog, by voice and by gestures. They may be used in combination or singly. In certain cases the gesture accompanying the vocal command is most effective. In general, however, I place more reliance on spoken orders than on gestures. There are times when the latter are useless; in the dark, or when you do not have the attention of the animal, gestures will do no good at all. It is quite all right to use hand and arm signals as an aid, but first of all make sure that the dog responds to your voice.

Give commands firmly and very clearly. To obey you, your dog must understand what you are saying. Use as few words as possible, and say them in the same way each time.

Training lessons should be short — fifteen or twenty minutes at the most. For the beginners, the pups, about ten minutes is all they can take. When the lessons are drawn out too long the dog will lose all interest and won't even try to do your bidding.

If you have the time to give several lessons each day, say morning, noon, and night, your pupil will progress faster than if he only gets one chance a day. Short sessions, repeated often, are the keys to steady improvement.

In hot weather you should not try to get as much work from the dog. I always lighten up on training during hot weather, and eliminate it entirely through the hottest part of the midsummer days. Dogs feel the heat more than we do, I am convinced, and will never work their best. I have found it worthwhile to start training early in the morning during the hot months, relax during the heat of the mid-day, and resume again after the sun begins to lower.

PRAISE AND REWARD FOR GOOD WORK

Because most dogs, most of the time, are eager to please their masters, it is very important that the trainer show the dog that he is pleased with it when the work is carried out successfully. When you give your dog an order and he shows that he is trying to obey, he rates praise for his effort. If he fails to carry out the command to your entire satisfaction he still is entitled to your praise *if you can see that he tried his best*. When he is shown that he pleased you by his performance he will try even harder the next time.

There are several ways for you to show your dog that you approve of his actions. You can use any one of them or a combination:

1. Praise and pet him. Most dogs love to have their master tell them what good dogs they are. Use a warm, friendly tone of voice, and pet the animal as you talk.

2. If you can be sure that your dog won't run away you can let him get off his leash and enjoy a few minutes of romping with you. This is always good at the end of a successful lesson.

3. Reward him with a tidbit or two. This is very effective and will work well in practically all cases. There is one drawback. If he gets used to receiving one for work well done, you must be sure to keep them on hand so that you do not disappoint him.

HOW TO CORRECT MISBEHAVIOR

I do not believe that a dog must be punished physically for refusing to mind, or for failing to carry out commands, even though such failure is the result of stubbornness. There are other and better ways.

Since a dog values his master's good will the most of anything, it is a real punishment for him to be deprived of this. Scolding, accompanied by scornful looks, and given in a tone of voice calculated to shame the animal, will most always be very depressing to him. A dog quickly senses his master's attitude toward him, and if it is one of disapproval, he will realize it.

It is often effective to send a dog to his bed when he has disobeyed in some manner. Send him there and tell him he is a bad dog! Put your heart into telling him this — make him know that you mean it.

Never correct any animal in a spirit of reprisal; to reprove and to encourage a better performance are the only allowable reasons. If a dog does not follow my orders it is likely to be because he does not know how or because he is confused, and I try to correct him and make it clear exactly what I want him to do. But there are times when a dog may be feeling tough or "ornery," lazy or bored, and simply refuses to obey a command which I am sure he can handle because he has done it many times before. When this happens I change the command to some other routine, quickly, catching the dog off guard and forcing him to obey this new command at once. Then I take quick advantage of this act of obedience and praise him highly, thus establishing, once again, our normal good relations. This gets the dog back into the pattern of obeying all commands as they are given. If he still refuses, however, I again switch to some simple command that I am very sure he will obey, and when he does I call it quits for the session, knowing that the chances are that he will be in a better mood for the next lesson.

When reprimands are called for, there is only one time and one place for them to be given, and that is at once and on the spot, while the offense is fresh in the dog's mind. It is much worse than useless to correct the dog for some infraction of your rules which took place some time in the past. The dog will have no idea what he is being reproved for, and may even connect the punishment with some conduct which he has been taught was to be desired. He will become utterly confused unless all corrections follow at once the acts which merit them.

Dogs that are habitually punished long after the deed, are apt to develop in one of two unfortunate ways, depending upon the personality of the dog. The aggressive, bold animal will become bolder, tough and mean, while the shy or timid dog will tend to become so bewildered and unsure of himself that his spirit will be completely broken. Avoid both of these dangers by correcting your dog only at the time and site of his errors.

Never attempt to correct your dog unless he is firmly under your control. When training out-of-doors and correction becomes necessary, snap his leash on him at once. Off the leash he can run away from you, evade your eyes and reproving words, and be well on his way to picking up an entirely new and very bad habit. Remember, therefore, to make all corrections, other than incidental cautions, while you have your dog on its leash. This is fundamental. It follows, of course, that you must have the leash always at hand and ready when you conduct a lesson.

Never allow yourself to become angry with an animal. Any person should be ashamed of being unable to refrain from anger at a dog or other animal. If your dog misbehaves, or does not follow instructions, it may very well be that you are the one to blame for not making the directions or commands clear enough, or for having let poor conduct go unreproved at some time in the recent past. If, while training your dog, you find yourself losing control of your emotions, stop the lesson right there, and do not resume until you have completely recovered.

TRAINING AREA

The main requirement for a training area is privacy. No dog can give his best attention to his lessons if there are distracting sights and sounds competing with the master's voice.

Indoor training should only be given when you have the premises, or at least one room, to yourselves. If other members of the family or visitors are present it is highly unlikely that either you or the dog can give your best efforts to the job. One of the basic essentials consists of clear, firm enunciation of commands by the trainer and undivided attention of the dog to these sounds. So you should select a time when you and your pupil can be alone in some part of the house to conduct the lessons.

If you have a choice of outdoor areas in which to work select one which will be free from other activity. A back yard may be fine. A secluded section of a nearby park might be used. If such places are not readily available you may still have comparative solitude by choosing your times carefully. Probably certain periods of the day will find your outdoor area without distractions, and if you are free at such times your problem is solved. (Later, of course, you will want to test your dog, to see how well he knows his manners. For such times you will *want* activity and distracting interruptions.)

I want to warn you right here against trying to show off your pupil's accomplishments too soon. It will happen, I know from my own experience, that your dog will appear completely stupid if you try to make him go through his training routine before a perfect response to each command has been thoroughly drilled into his consciousness. It's all right, even desirable, to perform before others when you think you are near your goal of perfection with any one command. But do this only as an experiment, without great expectations, and be prepared to find that your dog is more interested in the spectators and what is going on around him than he is in your directions. This type of testing is entirely feasible, and quite different from seriously putting your pupil through his paces

Do you want an alert, happy, and useful dog? Train him! A dog is only half a dog until he has been given a course in obedience. Instead of having a spoiled, aimless, and unhappy pet, you'll own an animal you can be proud, a true companion.

before he is ready for it.

All in all, conduct most of your lessons in as quiet and secluded an area as you can conveniently find.

One Instructor or Several?

The ideal way to train a dog is to allow but one person to work with him. I know that this is the fastest way to get on with the job, assuming, of course, that this person is qualified as a trainer. I don't mean that this person must be highly experienced; I do mean that he must like to train the animal, he must have patience, and to quote the old joke (which actually isn't a joke) "he must be smarter than the dog."

The reason for the preference for one-person training is simple. The dog will have a hard enough time at first in trying to understand what it is all about, and a great deal of repetition will be necessary. Unless the commands are always given in the same way, and preferably in the same tone of voice, he will have difficulty in connecting them with the action desired by the trainer. Now it is obvious that one person is much more likely to give the orders in the same way and to make them always sound the same than two or more individuals will be able to do. Therefore, if it is possible, one member of the household should be delegated as trainer-in-chief. Later, when the pupil is familiar with his role, it will be all right, even desirable, for others to take a turn at the job.

Do not misunderstand the above advice. Just because one person of the family should be the chief trainer does not mean that the others should pay no attention to what is going on, or should ignore the basic rules of dog training. For instance, if the dog is being taught to stay off the furniture by one person it will be folly for another to allow the dog to get up on chairs or beds. All will have to be consistent.

However, just because it is best for one to assume the role of chief trainer, does not mean that two or more can't join in the job. If this is necessary, or if others want to have a hand in it, it can be done all right. In this case have a meeting and discuss the job about to begin. Agree on the order of lessons to be taught, the use of words, the method of handling the animal, and, as far as possible, the tones of voice to be used. Then stick to these "rules." This will work fairly well, and, indeed, will have one real advantage over the one-man sessions. This will be that one person will not undo what the other is trying to accomplish. Besides, training the family dog is fun, family fun, and is one more link in the strong group ties.

Is There Any Special Order of Lessons?

No, there is not a "required" order of procedure. You may, if you wish, jumble up the order as it appears in this book. As a practical matter, however, the sequence as given here does seem to work out well. Housebreaking should be started as soon as the dog is brought into the home. The use of the command "No!" should also be begun soon after the new family member arrives on the scene. Commands such as HEEL, DOWN, and STAY, also flow logically one after the other. However, there is nothing to prevent you from switching the order around if you feel that you can do better that way. I certainly do not claim that the order that I use is the only sensible one. One caution, though: Do not try to work your dog off-leash in any routine until he has mastered the command while on-leash!

What Is the Best Way to Conduct a Lesson?

I think that I can best answer this question by listing some dos and don'ts that I always follow. (By the way, don't think that I'm bringing up too much technical matter here. Most of this advice is simply common sense, which you would use anyway. I have merely listed it in convenient form.)

TRAINING TIPS

1. Make each lesson short, fifteen or twenty minutes is enough. Conduct the lesson briskly, in a business-like manner.

2. Don't try to train a dog immediately after his meal. At least an hour should intervene.

3. Give the dog some exercise before starting. He should have ample opportunity to relieve himself before starting work.

4. Give all commands in a firm, brisk tone of voice. Speak loudly enough to be easily heard.

5. Always start off by reviewing an earlier lesson. Praise the dog for doing this correctly, thus starting in a pleasant way.

6. Conduct lessons in privacy; if this is impossible please ask those present to be as quiet and unobtrusive as possible.

7. Never let your pupil ignore even one of your commands. If he does, repeat it if it is one with which you know he is familiar. If not, repeat it and show him what it means, meanwhile giving the command over and over again.

8. Use as few words as possible. Don't say, "I want you to STAY right here." Say "STAY!"

9. Always end each lesson by letting your dog know that he is doing all right. By this I mean that you should end up by having the dog do some one thing correctly, so that he wins praise and encouragement at the end. If, in order to accomplish this, you have to revert to some simple command that he does well, do this. Don't build up any sense of frustration in the dog. Let the dog see that correct behavior wins your praise.

10. Don't expect your dog to learn too fast. Some dogs do pick up their lessons very quickly, but others are slower at learning. (Some teachers aren't as good as some others, too, don't forget.)

11. Be reasonable about the whole business. During hot humid weather lighten up on the training activities. Neither pupil nor master are apt to be at their best.

12. If the dog shows any signs of being ill do not attempt to bother him with training work. Lack of appetite, dejected appearance, "runny" eyes or nose, refusal to play or act in usual manner, are symptoms of ill health and call for a check-up by the dog's vet.

"NO!" IS A VALUABLE COMMAND

The simplest command your dog will ever respond to is the word NO. It is also one of the most valuable in controlling him. From puppyhood to his old age this command will do a great deal to keep him in line. This being true, you should begin the use of this word right at the outset of your dog's life in your household.

There are two things that you should know about the use of this word. One is the way it is to be used. The other is the absolute obedience by the dog which it requires. The word is to be used whenever your dog does anything that you do not want him to do. The instant he starts to "act up" in any way tell him, very sharply, "No! No!" If you are dealing with a puppy who has had no training yet you will have to show him what you mean by your word NO. If he has jumped up on a chair you should put him down on the floor as you continue shaming him with the word NO. If he is chewing a piece of furniture, someone's shoe, or anything else of value, take it away from him as you sternly tell him "No! No!" He will soon associate the use of this short but very firm command with the correct idea — the fact that it means to stop whatever it is that he is doing.

In giving this command don't make it a weak one; snap it out to show that you mean it, and no foolin'. You can't afford to have your pet ignore its meaning. He must obey, at once. In fact, one of the objects of training your dog is to impress upon him the fact that he must

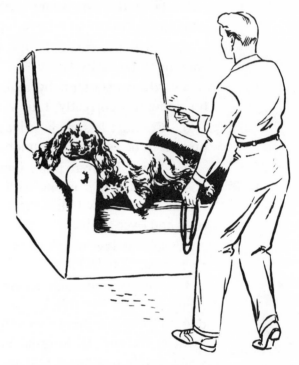

The word "NO" is the best friend the dog owner has — indoors or out.

obey you in all ways. It must be so impressed upon him that he will come to realize that he has no alternative to obeying. As this command "No!" is a simple one, it reasonably follows that it is one which can be used to teach the power of your control. If you tell the dog NO be sure that he minds. Do not let him ignore it, even once.

As soon as you have your puppy or grown dog minding you when you use this command you have passed an important milestone in the training routine.

"GO TO YOUR BED" USED AS MILD PUNISHMENT

In addition to a dog's bed being a place for him to sleep, it serves two other important purposes. One is that it is a place of refuge for him. When the cares of the dog world get a little too much for him he can retire to his bed and brood about the whole business. It is his private spot, his castle.

The third purpose of a dog's bed is more for the benefit of the owner than of the dog. It is a place to which the owner can confine the dog when necessary or desirable. When, for any reason, you want your dog out of the way, you should be able to tell him to go to his bed and have him do so at once. When the dog has misbehaved you can send him to his bed, and make him stay there, as punishment. This is very effective in most cases.

To serve all three of these purposes as well as possible, you should place the bed in some out-of-the-way place. In addition to being out of drafts, dampness and high heat, it should be removed from busy family activities. The more solitude and quiet you can furnish your pet, without relegating him to a lonesome room all by himself, the better. In other words, if the dog has a quiet corner to himself, out of the family's way, yet cozily arranged so that he can still keep an eye on their doings he will indeed be well taken care of in this respect.

For the first few days, or until he knows the meaning of the word BED, it will be wise to keep him fastened to or near the bed for a part of each day. When you take him to the bed repeat the word a dozen or more times. As you do this day after day he will come to connect the two, the word BED and the bed.

As soon as he knows the meaning of the word you can train him to go there at your command. Put his collar and leash on him. Tell him, "GO TO BED!" If he starts to obey right away you've got a very smart dog. More likely he won't know what you mean at first. So you'll have to show him. Giving sharp little jerks on his collar, steer him to his place, repeating the command over and over.

Don't try to drag him along — ever. Repeated jerks on the leash, not a steady pull, are to be used.

When you think the dog has learned his lesson, try sending him to the bed by command only — don't take him there. If he obeys, fine. If not, start over again with the leash.

It will be a help if his bed is comfortable for him. The mattress should be clean, slightly soft, and never allowed to remain lumpy. Also the bed should be large enough for the dog to stretch out in, turn from side to side in, and otherwise get good relaxing rest.

If you fasten the dog to or near his bed, be sure to use a light chain instead of leather, fabric or plastic which he can chew to pieces. Once your dog finds that he can chew his way to freedom you have created an unnecessary problem for yourself.

"HEEL," THE FIRST BASIC COMMAND

As a prelude to teaching your dog to HEEL, you should put a collar and short leash on him and let him drag it around for a day or so. By doing this he will not be frightened when he first feels its pressure on his neck as you guide him through his first lesson in this command.

The goal here is to train your pet to walk quietly at your side, matching his gait to yours, neither preceding you or lagging behind.

You should teach your dog to do this in two ways, on his leash, and off. In both versions of the command he should act in the same manner, that is, he should walk without being forced and without urging, at your left side, with his right shoulder being about even with your left knee. Obviously those dog and owner combinations which you often see on the street conducting what might pass for a tug of war have no conception of the way a dog should act when walking with his master. The dog should never pull against his leash. He should keep up with his companion, adjusting his pace whenever necessary.

You must use the dog's choke collar and short leash in training him. First put the collar on him. See the pictures of the correct way to put this on. Then snap the leash on the collar. Next, take your stance beside the dog. Either step over to put yourself on his right side or pull him around to your left. (After the first lesson you should stand and make him be the one to find the correct position.) Hold the end of the leash in your right hand, and let it run through your left. Form a circle with your left thumb and fingers and let the leach run loosely through this circle. By this type of hold you can allow the dog slight freedom, yet can tighten up instantly.

The right way to put a choke collar on your dog.

The wrong way, except when teaching the dog to go DOWN.

The dog should stand and walk so that he is close to your left knee. Whether you want him to be exactly even with your knee or a little ahead or behind is a personal matter as long as you are not training for obedience competition. Whatever position seems to be the most natural or comfortable is the one you should adopt. The pictures on page 41 show the correct stance of dog and handler in obedience competition work, and if you have any idea that you might want to go as far as this with your training you should start in with this correct stance.

Now for the first action. Start forward, and as you do so command, sharply, "Duke, Heel!" or whatever the dog's name may be. If he gets

Two views of the correct position for a dog at HEEL. There is nothing wrong with having your pet walk on your right side if you prefer it, but this is the usual stance for dog and handler.

When the dog gets ahead, or drags behind, jerk him to your side.
DON'T PULL — JERK! This is a very important point.

Too far to the side is as bad as too far ahead or behind. It is also wrong to let the animal sniff along the ground as you proceed.

under way that is fine, even though he may start off with a rush as though trying to pull you right along with him. For this first lesson or two it doesn't matter very much how he acts; you are doing little more than getting him used to walking with you, on his leash. If you walk long enough to tire the dog slightly this is so much the better because he will not be quite so frisky and will naturally tend to stay a little more at your side. On these first few walks repeat the command HEEL often, especially as you give the leash sharp jerks to bring the dog to your side from either behind or ahead.

Do not, under any circumstances, pull him along. Don't pull him back to you, or pull him up to you from behind you. Bringing a dog along by a steady pull on the leash is very sure to develop him into a "puller." You see them every day on the street, the dog pulling and panting, and the owner following with outstretched arm trying to keep up. If your dog refuses to walk, or if he walks too fast, check him by a series of sharp jerks on the leash, hard enough to get the result you want. You won't hurt the dog's neck, because he will give in to you long before he is injured. And by this jerking motion you will not start him in a bad habit — the jerks continue until he minds and then they stop. He soon learns that obeying your commands is an instant way to stop the uncomfortable jerks on his neck.

After one or two walks with your pupil you will begin to exact a little precision from him. Make him tend to business a little better. Don't let him wander quite as much. Bring him to your side more often, and more sharply. Repeat the verbal command every time you do so.

Give him slack in the leash whenever he comes to the correct position, then if he starts to edge forward too fast, or to drop behind, speak to him quickly, "HEEL, HEEL!" If this reminder is enough to make him mind you will know that you are making progress. But if he pays little or no attention to your words you'll have to remind him very forcibly by a few snappy jerks on the leash.

This command should not be difficult for the dog to catch on to fairly quickly. One thing that will delay his mastery of it will be sloppiness on your own part. If you are not vigilant in keeping him in the correct position, once the first lessons are over, he will not know for sure that the word HEEL calls for absolute obedience — for him to walk EXACTLY where you have shown him. You must spend every minute of the later lessons in keeping him walking precisely at your side.

When you have finally arrived at the point where you have perfect obedience by your dog while he heels when on his leash, you are ready to complete the job. This means that he must work just as well when off leash as he does when the leash is on. This is quite a step, but if the first part has been drilled into him sufficiently well it will not be difficult to keep him heeling perfectly without the restraint of the leash.

The procedure is the same, except that you eliminate all preliminaries. He must mind from the beginning. Even though he is working without the leash he must have the choke collar on his neck. This is so that you can instantly snap the leash on if necessary. And it will be necessary if he does not mind you when you tell him to HEEL. Off the leash his manners should be just as good as they were on it. His position at your side must be just as precise. At first he may wander slightly but he should respond at once when you remind him where he belongs. If he doesn't you will know that he still needs more training.

The ordinary dog can be so well trained in this command that when he has completed his work he will stay correctly at his trainer's side even though seriously distracted by sights and sounds of heavy traffic on the streets. When your dog reaches this stage you will take real pride in taking him for walks with you.

TRAINING SUGGESTIONS

1. This is the first lesson to be taught out of doors, and the first having to do with other than house behavior. Therefore it is well to see that it is done correctly. I have noted that dogs which learn this first obedience command well, tend also to do well with the balance of their training. This is one of the easiest commands for a dog to learn, and it seems to be that success in this one causes them actually to like training work.

2. Do not let the dog walk with his head down, sniffing as he goes. If he tries to do this jerk him up. He should carry his head up in the air and walk in an alert and willing manner.

3. Your dog should adapt himself to your changes of direction and pace. When you turn — either way — the dog must also turn, instantly. On turns to the left the dog must slow down slightly, and on right turns he must speed up a little. If you step backward or sideward the dog must do the same, without delay.

4. HEELING is not a strenuous exercise, and you can give your dog longer lessons in it than in the other commands.

Well behaved dogs will sit quietly at their master's orders. Strolling with a dog isn't much fun unless he has been trained to have good manners.

"SIT," IS EASILY TAUGHT

Next upon the schedule for your dog is learning the meaning of the command to SIT. Just as in the previous lesson you start this one by putting the choke collar and short leash on the dog. Indoors or out, find a private place for this lesson, one where you can have the dog's complete attention for ten or fifteen minutes.

As a starter walk around a minute or two with the dog at HEEL. When he does this well praise and pet him. Then, on this good note, start on the new task.

The choke collar should be arranged close up behind your dog's ears. Now, walk forward a few steps with him at HEEL. After a few steps, stop, grasp the leash close to the collar, say "Sit!" and pull upward smartly with your left hand, and at the same time press down on his hind quarters with your right hand. This forces him to SIT. Repeat, over and over again, the command. All of the action takes place simultaneously, the command, the upward jerk of the leash, and the downward push on the dog's back.

If the dog attempts to lie down, instead of SIT, jerk up on the leash, telling him to SIT. Keep him in the correct position for a minute or so while you tell him many times to SIT.

Again resume your walk, with the dog at HEEL. Take but a few steps and repeat the whole procedure all over again. Keep this routine up for ten or fifteen minutes, a long enough lesson for the first time.

Up to this point I haven't said anything about how and where the dog should SIT. You have enough trouble at first in just getting him to SIT at all. But, as in most things, there is a right

way and a wrong way. The right way is for the dog to SIT facing the same direction as his handler, with his head about even with the handler's left leg, and about six inches away. These directions apply, of course, when the dog is told to SIT while HEELING with his trainer. At other times he will be expected to SIT in other positions.

At first you'll have to help him to SIT in the proper position. As you command "SIT!" he should, after being shown a number of times, attempt to obey. If he does it correctly that is fine. But probably some of the times, if not most of them, he will SIT facing in any way but the right one — facing the front, close to your leg. When he starts to SIT in any other position you can help him to do it right by using your left hand to reach over and swing his rear to the left or right as need be. If he tries to SIT too far ahead of or behind you, jerk him by the leash to the correct spot. If his head and shoulders are where they should be but his hindquarters are at an angle, swing him around with your left hand. It will be easier to do this as he is settling down than to change him after he is seated.

Your goal is to have your dog assume the correct sitting position promptly whenever you give the command. If he is walking he must SIT at once. When you resume your walk, your dog must, without further command, get up and resume heeling, unless he has been commanded to STAY, a command described a little later in this book.

As soon as your dog will SIT whenever you tell him to do so while you have him on the

As you give the command to "SIT," you must jerk up on the collar and press down sharply on the dog's back. These actions force obedience.

leash, you may try the same command while he is off his leash. This is the real test of how well he has learned the lesson.

Don't forget to praise the dog when he performs this act as he should. That's what he works for, you know. When he does a good job at your command be sure to pet and praise him well. On the other hand, when he does not do well, and refuses to cooperate, punish him by voice, telling him what a bad dog he is, shaming him, and by sharp jerks on the leash.

Once the dog has thoroughly learned this command you will be able to make him SIT any place and any time, merely by giving him the order. There is another way of finishing up this lesson. This is to train your dog to SIT immediately, without being commanded specifically to do so, whenever you stop walking. Many people like this. To show the dog what you want, it is only necessary for you to press him into the SIT position each time you interrupt the HEEL exercise by halting. When you resume your walk the dog should at once take up his position at your side.

This command, SIT, is used many times, of course. I have spoken of it here only in terms of using it when the dog is at HEEL. However, once the command has been learned by the dog it can be used under any circumstances. When the dog is told to SIT that is what he must do, on or off leash, indoors or out.

"DOWN," IS IMPORTANT FOR CONTROL

In teaching a dog to go DOWN it's a good idea to show him, the first few times, just what you mean by this command. Gently pull his front legs out from under him as you press down with your right hand on his back.

Next on schedule for your dog's education is the command "DOWN!" If he has learned the lessons up to this point without too much trouble this one should be the easiest. Each new command gets easier; the dog tries harder, as he learns what is expected of him, and even though he tackles commands which present more difficulties they are learned faster. Even in dog training "Nothing succeeds like success."

Make your dog SIT, at your left side. To get off to your usual good start, praise him effusively when he does this correctly.

Of course your dog will not know, right off, what the command DOWN means, so you will have to show him. Drop to your left knee. With your left hand gripping the leash close to the

*After he knows what this command means, jerk him to the correct
position, until he will assume it at your command.*

If you want to save wear and tear on your legs and knees you can use this method to force the dog into position. Pull up sharply on the leash, which passes under your foot.

dog's collar, give it short, sharp jerks downward. Say, "DOWN, DOWN, DOWN." Repeat this several times.

Some dogs are stubborn about this, and are inclined to argue with their trainer about going DOWN. In this case the trainer must try again and again. If your dog simply refuses to obey you can make him cooperate by using your right hand to pull his forefeet out from under him while at the same time giving the command and jerking downward with your left hand on the leash.

It helps to give the command often, even during the time the dog is actually DOWN. The dog can't hear it too often while he is learning.

There is another method of teaching this command, one which saves the trainer a lot of stooping and bending. Again make your dog SIT at your side. Lower the leash, holding it in your right hand. Now put the instep of your

left shoe over the leash. Give the dog the command, "DOWN!" As you do so, force him to obey by lowering your left foot on the leash and at the same time pulling on it with your right hand. Repeat this over and over until the animal understands and obeys instantly.

After enough lessons have been absorbed by the dog so that he understands and obeys this command willingly, you may teach him to respond by a gesture as well as the spoken command. It is not important that you do this, but often it will be a help if he knows both the verbal and hand signal for DOWN. Even so, your main reliance should be on the spoken command, "DOWN!"

With this command, as well as the previously taught SIT, your dog must instantly get up and HEEL when you start to walk away, unless you order him to STAY.

TRAINING SUGGESTIONS

1. Obeying this command seems to have a depressing effect on most dogs. It is not a good idea, therefore, to keep them at it for long at a time. Also be sure to give your pet plenty of praise and petting when he does a good job of it. End each session with some exercise or play that he enjoys.

2. In teaching this command vary the routine. That is, don't always give the commands in the same order so that your dog will come to think that they should and always will come in the same sequence. As soon as he knows the meaning of DOWN, you should make him obey it at times other than when he is HEELING. Surprise him with this command at odd times around the house or yard. You want this order to be obeyed instantly, no matter where or when it may be given.

3. When the dog has gone DOWN from the HEEL position he should be facing forward, just as he was when he was walking.

4. Until he is letter perfect in obeying this command the dog will try to get up as soon as you release pressure on the leash. Keep him there, though, by repeated jerks on the leash as you say, "DOWN, DOWN, DOWN!"

5. At this time it will be wise to repeat work on the SIT routine. While he is DOWN, give the order to SIT. If he does not obey this at once, as he should, pull him up by jerking quickly on the leash. This, too, do over and over again.

6. When you pet or praise your dog for responding to the word DOWN do it only after he has gotten back to his feet. While he is DOWN it is not a good idea for him to be petted by anyone, including yourself. If you put him DOWN and then make a fuss over him and tell him "That's a good boy!" or give him similar encouragement he'll want to get right up again. Make it a definite rule that he should not be petted by anyone when he is obeying this command.

7. This business of putting the dog DOWN has an additional function beside the apparent one. Most dogs do not like this command and obey it reluctantly. You may take advantage of this. When at any time in the future your pet gets careless in obedience in general and shows a tendency to disregard your orders, or obeys only in a slow and sloppy manner, just rehearse this DOWN exercise over and over again. It really shows the animal which one of you is the master. When he finally performs it well several times in a row you will no doubt find that he is once again a well trained dog in all ways. This command carries great authority over a dog.

"STAY," IS OFTEN USED

As soon as your dog has conquered his DOWN lesson it is time to teach him to STAY, the next in this series of control commands.

Again start out by putting the dog on his short leash. After reviewing a few previous lessons make him lie DOWN. Now tell him to STAY. This will be easier understood by the dog if you accompany the spoken word by a restraining gesture. While facing him raise your right hand to approximately the level of your eyes, and point your index finger at him. Keep your hand in this position while you repeat the command over and over again. The combination of gesture and spoken order is very effective, much more than either one alone. Of course as this is a new and unfamiliar word he won't be apt to STAY at all, but will proceed to get up at once when you walk away a few steps. Each time he attempts to get up you should command him to go DOWN again, then to STAY.

After one or two fifteen minute lessons he will probably STAY while you walk around him, at the end of the short leash. Then back away from him, step over him, and otherwise test him out.

Next, if he is doing well while you have him STAY while he is DOWN, have him SIT and STAY. Repetition will again teach him what you want.

When you have demonstrated that he is proficient when worked on the short leash you can go through the same routine with the dog on his long leash. Start off by making him lie DOWN at your left side. Roll up all of the surplus length of this leash in your hand and then throw it out away from you. (The snap

end is attached to the dog's collar, of course.) Now command him to STAY, repeating yourself several times. Then turn away from him

A quick way of putting the idea across to your dog is to place him on a dog mattress, a box, a small rug, or any object which tends to give him a feeling of restriction. This little trick can save you hours in the teaching of this command.

and walk to the free end of the leash. Turn and face him. Repeat the word STAY. Hold out your hand toward him in the gesture of STAY. If he rises you must rush right back to him and make him lie DOWN again, and then go back to the end of the leash. Your objective at this time is to have the dog STAY, DOWN, quietly while you walk from him to the far end of the leash, pick it up and face him, and remain there for several minutes. Keep working on this problem until he will STAY without question.

Both the vocal and gesture commands are used in training a dog to STAY. This is one command you must teach with great patience — even the best dogs get nervous at it.

Go out of the dog's sight, but stay in the vicinity, in some spot where you are able to observe the dog and force him back if he tries to leave.

The next step in this exercise is to train your dog to STAY at your command when you are out of his sight. It may work out well to try this, at first, in the house. Pick a quiet room, well away from other family activity, to work in. Put your dog DOWN, order him to STAY, and leave the room. If you can arrange it some way, watch him, possibly through the crack in the door if it is not quite shut. If you see that he show signs of nervousness and is about to get up, go in to him and repeat the command very sharply. If he has already gotten up make him lie DOWN again and repeat the word STAY several times.

At first leave him alone for only a minute or so at a time. As he gets better at it, and shows less tendency to want to get up and follow you, gradually increase the time involved until you are leaving him for as long as ten minutes. Each time you come back and find that he has obeyed you, have him SIT and then praise and pet him. If you give a treat for good behavior allow one after every good performance like this.

When you feel that it is time to try the same test outdoors find a secluded place. Attach the long leash to the dog's choke collar. Then fasten him by this to a stake or tree in the yard. This will allow you to work freely but will also assure that the dog can't run away from you. If he is an older dog and you are sure that he won't take advantage of freedom to wander away you won't need to fasten him at all.

Start the practice in the same way you did in the house. Make him lie DOWN and tell him to STAY.

Now, after several warnings to him to STAY, go away from the area. Behind some bushes or around the corner of the nearest building will do — any place that you are hidden from the dog but where you can still observe his actions.

Watch him. The instant he gets restless and starts to get up you must rush back to him, make him go DOWN again and order him once more to STAY. Each time use the gesture as

well as the verbal command. While you are out of his sight he may start to chew the leash. If he does, go to him at once, tell him NO very sharply and if this is repeated again shake him by the nape of his neck as you scold him. As soon as he gives in to this command and will STAY quietly while you are out of sight you are near the end of this lesson.

The final test of the ability of your dog to follow your instructions about STAYING will have to be staged with the help of a friend, preferably another dog owner. Fasten your pupil with the long leash again, even though he has graduated from it under ordinary circumstances. Now put him DOWN firmly, then command him to STAY, after which you should disappear, as you have done before in practice. Now, by arrangement, your friend walks by. He should stop near your dog. Does this make your animal get up? If so you quickly appear and scold him sharply. If he pays no attention, though, have your friend do more to annoy him. He should speak to the dog, coax him, and approach closer. If all this fails to goad your pet into getting up you have done an excellent job of training. If he does give way you will have to correct him and then give him some more lessons along the same lines. A final test might be to have the same person pass by with his own dog on leash. If this too fails to arouse yours to get up and investigate you have a well trained dog in this respect.

This command, making your pet obey you even though you are not at his side to enforce your will, is very important. The over-all effect it has upon him is to make him more obedient in all ways, to all commands. He will have the feeling that you know every thing he does, are everywhere, and that he must obey every order you give him.

A variation of this routine may come in handy occasionally. There may be times when you would like to leave your dog for longer periods, tied. Even though a dog is well trained in the STAY command it is not feasible to leave him on his own for five or ten minutes. Therefore all dogs should be taught to remain tied, without making a fuss of any kind, without barking or howling, and without chewing on the leash or tie rope.

To train yours to do this, fasten him to a stake, post, or tree. Use a light chain instead of some material which he could chew into pieces. Leave him and go out of his sight. After he has remained quietly for several minutes return and unfasten him. Praise and pet him. In succeeding lessons gradually lengthen the time you leave him alone and tied. As he begins to accept this without misbehavior of any kind, you can take a chance and leave him for an hour or two, still using the chain instead of a soft material that could be destroyed by chewing. (Once a dog finds out that he can free himself by chewing his bonds he can never be left tied with any certainty that he won't do it again.)

After a number of times when your dog has performed perfectly, you should change to his short leash and leave him in the same manner. He'll bear watching from your hidden vantage point for a while, but if he shows no desire to chew his way to freedom you can feel that this is another lesson well learned.

TRAINING SUGGESTIONS

1. After you have told your dog to STAY, and he is obeying, do not praise or pet him. If you should do this he will want to get up right away. If it helps him you may repeat the word STAY in a calm, soothing tone of voice.

2. Praise him for his good work only after he has been released from the STAY position. After he has been told to SIT or HEEL give him his reward.

3. A little trick that I use very successfully in training a dog to STAY is to place him on a low box, dog mattress, or even a number of old newspapers. Anything to make him feel "place conscious." Dogs seem to get the idea of STAY sooner if they have a "place" to STAY at first. Try this.

"COME," MUST BE LEARNED PERFECTLY

The teaching of this command follows immediately the successful completion of STAY. This is perhaps the most important of all in your dog's education. Nothing is more annoying than to have to call and call a dog to get him to come to you, or worse yet, be unable to get him to come even though you do call repeatedly. This is one of the most common complaints of owners. Fortunately, it is really easy to train a dog to come at once, on the double!

Start this with your dog beside you, his choke collar and long leash attached. Wad up the excess portion of leash and toss it out away from you. Make the dog lie DOWN, tell him to STAY. Now walk to the other end of the leash, pick it up, turn around and face the animal.

Wait a moment or two then call him, "Come" or "Prince, Come!" It sometimes helps a little to add the dog's name when using this command. The tone of your voice should be serious, commanding, not coaxing or wheedling.

If he does COME to you, pet and praise him for this. If he doesn't, and this won't be surprising, simply reel him to you hand over hand. Even when you have to pull him in in this manner you must still praise him for coming when he gets to you.

Practice this lesson many times. Soon he will understand what the word COME means and will act upon it at once. Then you can change the routine some. Leave his choke collar on him but unsnap and remove the leash from the collar. Now, with him in the DOWN position at your side, hold one end of the leash in one hand and throw the other as far from you as possible. Drop your end on the ground, tell the

With the dog at your left side, throw the free end of the long leash out away from you. Tell the dog to STAY, then walk to the end of the leash, turn and face the animal.

Call him to you. If he doesn't come at once you must jerk smartly on the leash. In later stages you can have the leash free of his collar, merely pretending to jerk him to you.

dog to STAY, and walk to the other end of the leash as you have done before.

When you turn to face him call to him just as you have been doing. He'll very likely COME, just as he has been in the habit of doing. But if he doesn't, bend over and pick up the end of the leash. Shake it a little, again command him to COME, and pull in the leash. Use a little showmanship here and over-play your motions as you pull it in. The dog will

think or assume that it is attached to his collar as it has been in past performances and will COME to you. If he doesn't, of course, you have been proceeding too fast and will have to drop back a little and practice making him COME while the leash actually is fastened to his collar. When he next seems ready for this step he may respond very nicely.

The final phase of this command, and the real goal, is to have your dog COME to you

Your dog must sit squarely in front of you when called in.
He should stay in this position until you tell him to heel,
at which command he must quickly get to your side.

when you call, without any physical pressure being involved. Go through the first part of the exercise just as usual, that is, have him SIT or lie DOWN (off leash) at your side, command that he STAY and walk away from him. Turn and face him as before, then call. If he is really ready for this step he will come at once. If he doesn't you'll have to forget this advance for the present and go back to the fundamental training of this command again.

Once this command is thoroughly learned your pet will COME to you the instant you call, no matter where he may be or what he is doing when you call.

To finish this lesson in good style, have the dog SIT in front of you when he reaches you. Do not pet him. Let him SIT there for two or three seconds, as this will nullify any tendency he might develop to jump up on you when called.

61

When he SITS, it should be right in front of and close to you. If he doesn't, reach out and grasp the leash close to the collar and back away, jerking on it and repeating "COME, COME," as you do.

After he SITS properly for a few seconds, command him to HEEL. As soon as he does this, the end of the sequence, you are free to pet and praise him.

ADDITIONAL TRAINING SUGGESTIONS

1. There is a right and a wrong way for your dog to execute this command. Even though he COMES to you at once he will still be wrong if he does it in a sloppy or sulky manner, or if he meanders slowly, sniffing along the ground as he approaches. The right way is for him to hurry it up, with his head in the air, and in an alert manner.

If you keep this in mind when you are at the stage of pulling the dog in and do this very briskly you will implant in his mind the necessity for speed in this maneuver. (A little tidbit when he arrives will help in the way he acts, too.)

2. Here is a very important caution: NEVER PUNISH YOUR DOG WHEN HE COMES TO YOU! Don't forget this. In teaching this command of COME never show displeasure when the dog COMES to you, even though he did it very poorly, even though he took too much time. You must not give him the idea that there can be anything worthy of punishment in coming to his master. You can speed him up as he is on the way by jerking on his leash, and verbally hurry him up, but when he gets there do not let annoyance goad you into berating him or showing displeasure. In teaching this command he must always be encouraged when he COMES to you.

(This caution applies also to any other time when your dog COMES to you at your direction. If he has done something for which he must be punished, do not call him to COME to you and then punish him. An owner simply cannot afford to show his dog that he may be walking right into punishment when he COMES to his master. Instead, in a case of this kind, you be the one to approach the dog, then snap his leash on him and punish him.)

3. I don't think that you should call your dog to you except when you really want him to COME. Too many people get in a habit of calling the dog, in a sort of half-hearted way, and then if the dog does not COME they do nothing about it. They'll call, "Here, Duke, COME here," and Duke pays no attention. But it wasn't important anyway, they make no protest when the dog disobeys, and the poor dog is farther away than ever from being a really well trained animal. If you call your dog to you for any reason at all, do it as though you meant it, in a forceful tone of voice, and INSIST that he obey you. The very first time he does not, get the dog's leash, go to him, snap it on him, and put him through a little refresher course in this phase of obedience. You will only have to do this once or twice if you are sincere about his manners, and if you never let him get by without obeying properly.

HOW TO DEAL WITH YOUR DOG'S BAD HABITS

The list of what we call bad habits of dogs is a long one and covers a very wide range of activities. Actually, "bad habits" is not an accurate way to describe most of these actions, because with few exceptions the behavior is "bad" only in the light of what the dog has been taught, or, in a great many instances, not taught. If you have taught your dog to stay off the furniture, but he persists in getting up on it whenever he is alone in the house, this is a bad habit. But if you encourage your pet to sit in chairs whenever he wants to do so this same act is not, of course, a bad habit. There is nothing fundamentally wrong with allowing a dog to use household chairs and beds for his comfort; it is just that most people don't like to have their furniture covered with dog hairs and soiled by a dog's feet. If you don't object to this behavior certainly the dog does not have a bad habit just because he takes advantage of your indulgence. Likewise, if you feed an occasional tidbit to him from the family dining table you can't say he has a bad habit if he begs food from the table at other times. It may be a habit all right, but the bad part of it is that you encourage it by an occasional bit of your food.

This is the way all of the dog's behavior pattern is formed. He has certain natural instincts which his owner should direct, encourage or repress. With careful thought you can instill good habits (the habits that are good for your home and for your way of living) in your dog, and you can also, and just as easily, prevent him from acquiring any of the so-called bad ones.

When you set out to control the behavior of a dog you should set up in your mind the pattern you wish your dog to follow. If you want to restrict your dog to certain rooms in the house decide this at once and never let him into the others, right from his first days with you. On the other hand, if you don't care where he goes in the house you won't need to give this any thought. Another example: If you like to have your dog sit in a chair with or beside you, or sprawl out on the beds, you won't be concerned about preventing such behavior. The list of behavior choices is long, and if you start early enough you can make the dog's own choices follow your training with little or no trouble.

You can control the behavior of your dog easily if you realize that the following steps are involved:

1. You must understand the causes of the undesirable actions of your pet.
2. You should know what preventive measures to use.
3. You must know how to change objectionable habits which your dog has already acquired.

As with all worthwhile projects a certain amount of real work is involved, especially in breaking habits which have gained control of the animal. However, the better your basic training of the dog has been, the easier your supplementary work will be. If he responds well to NO, HEEL, SIT, DOWN, STAY and COME, it will be relatively easy to mold his over-all manners.

The same handling will not gain equal results from all dogs. Some dogs are very smart, while some, I am sorry to say, are really not very bright. Some breeds are, on the whole, more intelligent than others. Some dogs must be handled very sternly, while others are so eager to please that they seem to try to anticipate your wishes. Some dogs are stubborn and these must be shown that they *must* obey, that there is no alternative. It is not uncommon to see dogs that are so timid, gentle, and shy, that they quail before a harsh word, even though they have been treated kindly all their lives.

So you'll have to get to know your dog. Study him. Experiment a little and find out what type of training gets the best results.

I thoroughly believe that it is unnecessary to punish a dog severely to gets its cooperation. I do feel that some dogs, but not many, must be treated roughly until they get it through their heads that their master is boss and what he says goes. But even what I call rough treatment is not the kind that is severe physical punish-ment. A harsh tone of voice in "calling down" the dog, a healthy shaking of the dog by its collar, and holding him by the collar and look-ing him right in the eye while "shaming" him, are generally all that are necessary by way of reproof. A dog that takes delight in being with his master can also be punished by being sent to his bed and made to STAY.

In trying to figure out why the dog disobeys you in any way, don't neglect to give considera-tion to the idea that he simply may not under-stand your directions — it may be that you are the one that is at fault. Everyone isn't a born teacher. Often we can improve our training skill by a little thought, plus trial and error. In general, most dogs like to please their mas-ters, so faults do not always lie with them. Examine your training methods before deciding that your dog is dumb or stubborn.

DESTRUCTIVE CHEWING CAN BE EXPENSIVE

DESCRIPTION OF THIS BEHAVIOR: The most natural thing a dog does is to chew every strange object with which he comes in contact. In most homes this is regarded as all right unless the object happens to be something of value that can be harmed by being chewed. When the dog brings a stick in and chews on this nothing is thought of it, but when he chews on the leg of a good chair it is termed destructive chewing.

CAUSE: Destructive chewing is very often the result of lonesomeness and boredom on the pet's part. He has nothing to do, no one to play with, so he picks up the first thing he comes across and starts to chew it up. Maybe he does it only as a means of passing the time, but maybe he really intends to destroy something in his pique at being left alone. No matter what the reason, the habit is annoying and can turn out to be very costly to the owner.

Puppies often chew anything handy because it feels good to them when their teeth are bothering them.

Some cases are the direct result of letting puppies play with old shoes, stockings, pillows or similar personal or household articles. Of course you later can't rightfully blame the same pup when he chews not the old shoes and other objects, but your best and newest ones. How can he tell the difference between the old and the new models?

PREVENTION: Buy your dog or puppy one or two toys to be chewed. Your pet supply dealer has any number of these on display. Be sure you get good ones that will stand a lot of mauling before coming apart. Veterinarians are often called upon to operate to remove bits of leather or rubber from the stomachs of dogs. High quality toys, well made of good materials, will stand a lot of abuse without coming apart.

Give one or two of such toys to your pet to play with and chew all he desires. Then, when you see him start to work on anything else, stop him at once. Tell him "NO!" Repeat it several times, then toss one of his own toys to him. Follow this procedure every time.

CURE: The cure for this bad behavior is just about the same as the preventive action. Take everything he should not have away from him — substitute these with his own toys. Scold him, give him the NO command, and shake him by the collar if he persists in bad chewing habits.

DOES YOUR DOG BARK CONSTANTLY?

DESCRIPTION OF THIS BEHAVIOR: If your dog barks (and keeps on barking) at every slight disturbance in or around your home he is what I call a constant barker. It is instinctive for a dog to bark, and most of us wouldn't want it otherwise. It is a good thing, except in rare instances, for a dog to bark once or twice when someone comes up on your porch, walks through your yard, or rings your doorbell. But once or twice is enough to give his warning, and then he should be quiet unless something truly extraordinary is taking place. But in such an event he should stop at once when told.

The incessant barker pays no attention to the command to stop. Bark, bark, bark, all day long, and often all night long also. This is annoying not only to you but to your close neighbors as well.

CAUSE: It is hard to generalize regarding this complaint. It is a fact that some dogs are very nervous by nature, and continuous barking is a manifestation of their nervousness. Other dogs are sometimes teased so much that they develop this bad habit. Some dogs are timid and shy and bark long and loudly at every sound and movement, inside or outside the house. I have known dogs that barked whenever they were left alone. On the whole I think that nervousness in one degree or another accounts for a large percentage of the trouble.

PREVENTION: Since it is natural for a dog to bark to give a warning of the approach of another person or animal to his home we should not try to halt such a reaction. But once the alert has been given we should not tolerate a continuation of it. After the dog has barked for a second or two, tell him, "NO." If he persists send him to his bed; talk very sternly to him, and make him STAY in his bed for some time.

No matter how young the pup is, be sure to squelch this excessive barking right from the start. By very small pups barking may not be too annoying, may even seem "cute," but it is from such small beginnings that full-fledged bad habits grow.

The prevention is to be vigilant in suppressing barking right from the first day in your home.

CURE: If the dog has respect for the command NO you may have no further trouble with him if you simply use this every time he continues to bark after the first couple of seconds. If the dog has graduated from your basic obedience course this will probably be all the reproof that will be necessary.

If the dog is not yet thoroughly trained, however, it will take more than a simple NO to make him realize that you are not going to allow him to continue his excessive noise. Put his choke collar and long leash on him. Arrange to have a helper in your job — possibly another member of the family. If the doorbell sets the dog off each time it is rung you should arrange to have your confederate ring the bell while you and the dog are in the house. Have the end of the long leash in your hand, but give the dog no sign or signal that anything is unusual. When the bell rings let the dog bark once or twice, then give him a sharp "No!" If he stops, well and good. If he keeps right on give the command once more and at the same time give a very sharp jerk on the leash, sharp enough to spin the dog right around facing you. Tell him "No, no, no!" He'll be surprised, ashamed, and puzzled. Repeat this experiment as many times as necessary. When the dog no longer gives more than a very few warning barks the battle is won.

GROWLING AND SNAPPING OVER FOOD

DESCRIPTION OF THIS BEHAVIOR: Some dogs are very ill-mannered when they are at their feed dishes, snarling, snapping and growling as they eat or guard their food. As a rule this bad habit is directly traceable to the dog's early days in the household. Probably it was teased at its mealtime, either by children, adults, or other dogs or the family cat.

If you have been around dogs very much, or have seen many of them in various homes, it is likely that you have run across at least one example of this annoying kind of canine. When his dish of food is set before him he starts growling and snarling between bites, and if anyone approaches he may even attempt to bite them. This type of behavior is very disconcerting, and can be dangerous as well.

CAUSE: Teasing a dog while it is eating will invariably cause it to become testy about this phase of its daily activity. I have seen cases where children were allowed to play with the dog while it was trying to eat. This certainly is not the time to bother a dog in any way whatsoever — his mind is on food, not play, and it breeds viciousness in him when he is disturbed.

If the dog is fed in the presence of other animals this may also have a tendency to make him guard his food in an overly zealous manner, although this is not always the case.

Another common cause of this bad behavior is allowing the dog to have a dish of food before him for a long time, even though he is not hungry enough to eat it. The old expression "A dog in the manger" is based on a true fact of canine personality. In most cases a dog will "guard" a dish of food for hours to prevent anything else getting it, even though he is not hungry and has no intention of eating it himself.

PREVENTION: This bad habit can ordinarily be prevented by the observance of two feeding rules.

The first rule forbids teasing the dog, especially during his mealtime. (Of course your dog should not be teased at any time, but we are here concerned specifically with the eating problem.) Under the heading of teasing comes bothering the animal in any way while he is intent on eating. Are you sure that no member of the family annoys the dog while he is feeding? Have you provided an area for the dog's exclusive use? This does not have to be large; two or three square feet will do nicely, but it should be located away from all distractions. The dog should not be forced to feel that he must protect his food — if necessary, any dog worth his salt would fight to guard his livelihood, so if you allow your dog to be goaded while eating you are solely to blame for resulting bad temper.

The second rule for preventing this bad behavior calls for offering the dog an adequate meal, at his regular feeding time, and then removing any·uneaten food after a reasonable interval. Even though the dog has plenty to eat, his nature urges him to protect any food remaining in his dish. Watch your dog's daily intake of food carefully and try to offer him only the amount needed to satisfy his normal appetite. Too much food tends naturally to make him put on weight to an unhealthy degree.

CURE: As with all other cures, regular obedience training will help to cure this unpleasant habit, and the perfectly trained animal will respond quickly to reproof when he understands what is expected of him.

If your dog's obedience training has not yet proceeded to the point that he will readily respond to commands with any high degree of consistency you will have to conquer this feeding fault by other means.

Change the feeding habits of your dog in all ways. First, arrange for him to eat in strict privacy, either in a room away from the stream of family traffic or in his regular place but at a time when he can have the room entirely to himself.

Put his regular dish of food before him with a cheery word of invitation such as "Here you are, Prince," and retire from the scene at once. After a reasonable length of time, maybe ten minutes, return and without a word pick up the dish, whether the food has been eaten or not. Do not let him get anything more to eat until his next mealtime. If he has been a confirmed grouch over his food dish, it is quite possible that he has enjoyed snarling, snapping, and guarding the food more than he has relished the actual eating. Letting him miss a meal or two will teach him to eat at once or go hungry.

After a period of eating alone, and in a limited time, your dog should mend his ways, especially if his obedience training in the other routines is proceeding in a satisfactory manner. A side benefit may also be that the dog will eat the food he needs for his well-being, but will not overeat because of a big dish of food being left before him for a long period of time.

ACTING UP WHEN LEFT ALONE

DESCRIPTION OF THIS BEHAVIOR: This bad conduct takes many different forms. When the dog is left in the house alone he shows resentment by acting in a manner which he knows to be wrong. He may bark or howl without let-up. He may chew up family possessions. Sometimes he may paw and scratch at the doors or windows. In extreme cases he may deliberately act as though he had never been house broken. In fact, these tantrums may be limited in variety only by the ingenuity of the dog — he will try any conduct he thinks will annoy the owner.

CAUSE: This type of behavior can be expected of a "spoiled" dog, a dog which has been babied too much, always being with the owner or others of the family, never having been taught from its early days that it must spend part of the time without human companionship.

PREVENTION: From the first days with a new pet dog make him spend at least one or two hours alone each day. If someone is always in the house you can get the same result by putting the dog in a room by himself for his isolation periods.

If he whines, barks, or cries during these early sessions ignore it; do not let your soft heart cause you to ease up and allow him to rejoin the family circle because of his lonesome cries. A day or two of this training will impress the newcomer with the fact that he must get used to spending part of the time alone.

CURE: While this appears to be a rather simple type of bad behavior it often turns out to be a stubborn one to cure. The fact that the misbehavior occurs in the owner's absence, rather than in his presence, makes it harder to effect a cure. Here again a basic obedience course is the best guarantee of success in breaking the animal of this bad habit of creating a disturbance whenever he is left alone. When the dog is completely obedient he will be in the habit of responding to any command which he understands, and the word NO should be enough to make him desist from acting up. But if he pays little attention to a simple command you will have to spend some time in further corrective measures.

Put the dog in a room alone, just as you do on the occasions when he acts in his "spoiled child" manner. This time, however, stay within easy hearing distance, although you should slam the outside door or in some way fool your dog into believing that you have left the premises. It is essential to make the dog think that he is all alone. If he is accustomed to have the run of the entire house when left alone you should go out as usual, but remain where you can easily hear when the commotion begins.

The moment the disturbance starts, pop into the house or the room, command the dog to stop by saying, "NO, Prince, NO!" Repeat this order several times, and after a short interval again leave the room. If the dog resumes his bad actions it will be your signal to break into his presence quickly once more and repeat your corrective commands. This procedure will no doubt have to be gone over time and time again before he will always behave as he should when staying alone.

If repeated commands and warning do not have the desired effect I think you will be justified in being severe with the dog. You can be quite sure that he knows he is doing wrong and is continuing out of spite. If you are getting nowhere by commands and shaming him, you will have to take him by the scruff of the neck and shake him as you tell him NO. Make him realize that you mean it, too.

DON'T LET YOUR DOG JUMP AGAINST YOU

DESCRIPTION OF THIS BEHAVIOR: This is one of those cases in which there is no serious harm done and the habit is not inherently "bad." Many people seem not to mind having their dog greet them by jumping up against them with their front feet. It is not unusual for dogs to be petted when they are stretched up this way against a person. This may be all right if the dog's paws are perfectly clean, or if the person's clothes won't be harmed by dirty dog paws. But if the dog is allowed to do this when his owner has on old or work clothes he certainly shouldn't be blamed if he does the same thing when the person is all dressed up or when the dog's feet are dirty. It is annoying to visitors to be greeted thus by the dog of the family.

If a large dog jumps up on a small child he may knock him down, with possible serious results, not the least of which can be a good scare for the child.

CAUSE: Dogs, or at least most of them, are eager to be petted by their masters. It is perfectly natural for them to jump up against a person in search of petting, and when this works, when they are petted if they jump up, the habit is started.

PREVENTION: Do not let your dog get started with this annoying practice. When he comes to you, either at your command or to welcome you home, command him to SIT as he reaches you. Let him SIT for a moment, then lean over and pet him. In other words, you go to him, instead of letting him come to you, for the petting which he craves. Petting, or similar recognition, is what he is after, so if he doesn't have to jump up on you for it he is entirely satisfied.

CURE: There are several accepted ways of

A nuisance, and rough on cleaning bills.

Step back quickly — don't give him a chance.

For most family dogs this behavior should definitely be regarded as undesirable, and subject to correction.

breaking this habit. The first one involves prevention of the act, primarily. Make it difficult or impossible for him to get his paws up on you.

If the dog persists in jumping up on you after he has been warned,
you can quickly show him that you won't stand for such conduct by
"kneeing" him. Use good judgment — don't be too rough.

Always be prepared to avoid this whenever he approaches you, keeping in mind what he probably will attempt to do. As he comes to you and raises his feet up jump back as quickly as possible, and at the same moment tell him, very sharply, "NO, NO, NO." Make him SIT, and remain that way for a minute or so, then lean over to him and pet and praise him. After a few of these experiences change the procedure a little. Now, instead of letting him attempt to jump up, lean over to him before he reaches you, stretch your hands out toward him, tell him to SIT, and pet him when he does. This method of breaking this habit will work only if everyone cooperates. If others of the family won't help you it will likely not work out.

Another way to show the dog that jumping up on people is taboo is to give his chest a good bump with one of your knees when he raises up. At the same time tell him, "NO, NO."

In breaking this habit you will find that if you have done a good job with your dog's regular training, so that he knows the meaning of NO, SIT, DOWN, and other basic commands, you can control him quickly merely by impressing upon him that this too is a command. When he starts to jump up on you the command "NO" must be obeyed.

THE RUNAWAY DOG IS A NUISANCE

DESCRIPTION OF THIS BEHAVIOR: There are two types of what may be called runaway dogs. One dog really runs away, that is, he leaves home at every opportunity and simply disappears, not returning until hunted up and brought back by his owner. The other type, not strictly a runaway, is the dog who wanders around the neighborhood, visiting other homes, begging food, annoying people, and often damaging shrubbery, gardens and

otherwise enclosed if they show any tendency to leave the owners' premises.

PREVENTION: Keep your dog under control. If he spends time out of doors keep him in a fenced pen or run-way if possible. If not, buy a tie-out stake and fasten him to this.

CURE: Don't give him any opportunities to get away from his home. Don't tie him up one day and neglect to tie him the next. Be consistent.

Confinement, indoors or out, is the best answer to the problem of the runaway dog.

other property. This dog, differing from the first type, returns to his home of his own volition after he tires of his visiting.

CAUSE: Owner neglect, primarily. I am thoroughly against letting a dog roam, and I believe that all dogs should be fenced, tied, or

Sometimes well-meaning neighbors make your task doubly difficult by feeding your pet tidbits when he manages to visit their homes. If so, tell them that you are trying to break him of the wandering habit and request their cooperation. Ask them to shoo him away when he appears at their doors, and refuse to feed him.

THE CAR CHASER IS A MENACE TO ALL

DESCRIPTION OF THIS BEHAVIOR: This habit of chasing cars is truly a bad one, from any angle, and there is actually no excuse for it. I am sure that you are familiar with it even though you have never owned a dog guilty of the offense. It happens frequently, in country or city, and is both annoying and dangerous. The dog may lie in wait for passing cars and then when one comes by he runs out and barks and chases alongside as far as he can keep up. Of course many dogs are killed at this pastime, and it has happened too many times that bad auto accidents have been caused by drivers being startled, swerving and losing control of their vehicles.

Another off-shoot is the chasing of motorcycles, scooters and bicycles. These operators too are placed in danger every time this happens.

This bad habit is strictly the dog owner's fault, and he should be held accountable for any damages sustained in resulting accidents.

CAUSE: If a dog is never allowed to run loose it will be impossible for him to pick up this habit. You should not allow your dog to run the streets alone. You should not allow him off leash on the streets even though you are with him, until he has completed a thorough course of obedience and will mind you under all circumstances.

Dogs on the loose may chase vehicles just for something to do; it must be exciting to them, a sort of game.

PREVENTION: Never let your dog run around the neighborhood alone. Never let your dog loose even though with you unless he will mind you instantly.

CURE: The most fundamental "cure" is to make it impossible for the dog to have a chance to chase cars. Do not let him roam. But if he is otherwise well-behaved and you like to let him lie and sun himself in the yard there are steps you can take to make this car chasing habit very unattractive to him.

One way that I suggest requires the cooperation of another member of the family or a friend. Equip yourself with a bucket of water into which some ammonia is mixed. With your helper driving, and you in the seat on the side to which your dog will run, go past your house

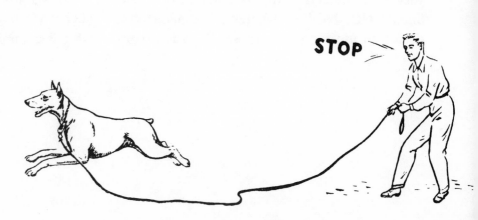

STOP

One or two surprises such as this will teach even the most confirmed "chaser" that he must find other ways to amuse himself.

or wherever it is that your pet lies in wait for his cars. Then, as he runs out and starts his chase, lean out and let him have the bucketful of water right in his face. As you do so shout "NO, NO, NO," at him. This should discourage him from repeating the act, although you may have to do an encore before he gets the idea that chasing cars isn't as much fun as he had thought it was.

Another possible way to cure your dog of this habit can be put into effect without a helper. Put the dog on his long leash. Take him to the spot that he has been using as his base for waiting for cars. When one appears, and he takes off in hot pursuit, you must be ready for him. Brace yourself. Let him go until he is very near the end of the long length of leash. Shout "NO, NO," or whatever command you decide to use for this purpose. If he is a con-

firmed car chaser the chances are that he will not heed your warning and will continue full tilt until he suddenly reaches the end of the leash. You are holding tightly to it and the result will be that he will give himself the surprise of his life. If he is going fast enough he may flip right through a summersault. One such experience may be enough to cure him completely of this bad habit, although several repetitions may be necessary to convince a stubborn animal.

The same type of lesson may be applied if your dog is an habitual chaser of any other type of vehicle, including bicycles.

I do urge you to regard this undesirable habit seriously and to take the remedial steps without delay when you first become aware that your dog is committed to it.

CURING THE BITER

DESCRIPTION OF THIS BEHAVIOR: There are two kinds of "biters." One is the dangerous, vicious dog that is downright ugly and a menace to his community. This type of dog is anti-social and there is little that the amateur trainer can do to change his attitude. We are not here concerned with this kind of dog. If your own dog has become a danger of this type you must keep him securely tied or fenced away from people. Better yet, put him in the hands of some proficient professional dog trainer. Many War Dogs, used in the war for attack purposes, have been successfully retrained to take their places in civilian life.

The other type of "biter" is the one which we are concerned with here. This is the dog which runs along beside a person and bites or nips at legs, skirts, or trousers, sometimes actually biting and sometimes merely going through the motions. In either case it is annoying, to say the least, and in those cases of actual bites it can be truly serious and dangerous.

CAUSE: Biting and nipping can be caused in a number of ways. Teasing your dog is an excellent way to start him toward this nasty little habit. The wrong kind of play is another. By this I mean letting a pup play by chewing, nipping, and chasing trousers, skirts, curtains, pillows or anything else that catches the youngster's fancy. It seems quite natural to play with a puppy by letting him chase after and bite an object, such as an old stocking drawn over the floor. It's fun, for you and for the dog. But as the dog grows he may start biting a little harder, and may not confine himself to the play sessions, but start chasing anything that moves. Then, next, he may show temper and anger when he is stopped and reproved.

PREVENTION: The best and surest way to prevent this bad behavior is never to let it get started. Don't instigate this type of play, and if your puppy starts it himself squelch it at once. This will mean stopping it even if some other member of the family or a visitor is the guilty person.

There are lots of ways to enjoy a dog without allowing biting. Throw a ball or a stick for him to chase and retrieve. Most dogs like to play hide and seek as well as children do. I do not advise playing tug-o-war with your pup, because this too is a game of biting. Biting and nipping is serious business and it is easier to prevent than to cure.

CURE: This bad habit must be broken as fast as possible. (If your dog is a biter, take my tip and keep your liability insurance up. Even a tiny dog that nips and bites can get his owner into serious trouble. Friends, neighbors, and passersby often look at the matter of a slight dog bite in a more serious manner than does a careless or indulgent owner.)

To cure this behavior you will have to do two things: Prevent him from having opportunities to bite people, and give him something else to do in its place.

Until a cure in this respect has been effected, do not allow the dog to be free to get near anyone. He should be kept in the house, or tied or fenced out of doors. When you take him for exercise keep him on his leash, and be ready to tighten up on it whenever the need arises.

In the house, if the dog is in the habit of taking it into his head to bite, you should keep one of his toys, say a rubber ball, handy. When the dog starts to run to you in the manner you recognize as one of his nipping moods don't walk away from him. Instead stop and lean over to him or kneel and hold your hands out to him. Pet him, praise him, and show him that because he didn't bite or nip (even though he had no chance) you are pleased. Hand him one of his toys, or just pet and talk kindly to him for a few minutes. Each time this happens will be one more victory over his urge to bite, and thus one step nearer a complete cure. It should be unnecessary to say that all members of the family must use this same treatment to assure breaking of the bad habit.

If, in spite of your efforts to outsmart him by bending down to play with him instead of letting him nip you, he continues to try, or if he bites your hands and fingers you will have to be harsh and firm with him. Use the word NO repeatedly. Snap his leash on him and take him to his bed, giving him sharp jerks as you do so.

Make him STAY at his bed, and if necessary fasten him right there. Do this each time he uses his teeth on you. With some dogs it will take quite a while to bring them to the point where you can depend on having them act as they should.

Never allow anyone to tease your dog. Many dogs have been goaded into mean and savage behavior, and children are not always to blame, either. Sometimes dogs that are tied or fenced outdoors are teased by people poking sticks at them, or by similar mean acts. This kind of treatment is more than some dogs can stand, and they get to hate all people. So, while you are working hard to break your dog of the biting and nipping habit you will do well to make sure that he isn't being encouraged in this type of behavior by others.

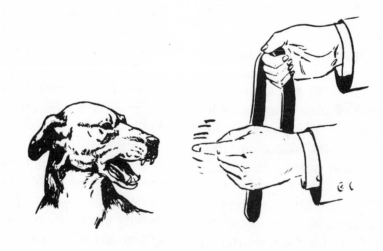

THE "FIGHTER" DOG

DESCRIPTION OF THIS BEHAVIOR: By calling a dog a "fighter" I mean a dog that is on the look out for dogs with which to pick fights. Despite the fact that it takes two to make a fight, it is generally a fact that one of the animals involved is an aggressor and the other a more or less innocent participant. It is the first one with which we are here concerned.

Most dogs are not addicted to looking for this type of trouble, and are content to go their way without in any way disturbing other canines. Some of these will stand up for themselves when set upon by a bully dog, while others will run away if possible, or, if they can't escape, will simply roll over and "take it." These dogs pose no problems for their owners as it will be rare or never that they become involved in fights.

Unfortunately, there are other dogs that fight just for the sport of it — or because they are either mean or have had some bad experience which has given their personality a bad twist. Some of these dogs are dangerous, often seriously injuring other animals; some are merely annoying, being bested in most of their fights, although still carrying a chip on both shoulders and attacking every dog they encounter, regardless of size or sex.

CAUSE: The possible causes for such anti-social action are many and varied. One or two breeds produce more than their share of these creatures.

Unless you have mistreated your dog, or have allowed him to be teased, it is probably a mystery why he has developed into a fighter, if that is the case. If this behavior quirk was simply born into him you will have to acknowledge it, be prepared for it, and know what to do about it.

PREVENTION: First, for a basic plan of action, your dog must be put through his obedi-ence lessons until he is as well trained as possible. In all but the most obstinate cases, perfect obedience manners will extend to this bad habit as well as to the more ordinary ones.

A second preventive measure is to keep your dog away from others. Don't let him run around the neighborhood alone.

The last rule, in dealing with a confirmed fighter, is to keep him on his leash whenever he is out of doors. Putting a muzzle on a dog will answer temporarily, but this is only a me-chanical solution, unsuited to use over a long period of time.

CURE: If general obedience training does noth-ing to cure a dog of the fighting urge you have a tough problem on your hands. If you can afford to turn your pet over to a professional trainer of wide experience this may be the best course of action.

One possible cure, which may or not work, is to get the cooperation of another dog owner who has the same problem — reforming a fighter dog. (It's not fair to try this with any other kind of dog.) Get a couple of spike training collars and put one on each animal, but put them on so that the spikes are turned out instead of in. Then bring the two dogs together and if they fall to fighting one or both may bite onto the upturned spikes. If so, this will possibly discourage them from this bad pastime. I don't have a lot of faith in this cure, but it has worked in some cases. A rigid obedience course is still, in my opinion, the best insurance against this and all other ex-amples of bad behavior.

I should caution you to keep calm if you are confronted with a dog fight. Most of these involve much more danger to a person attempt-ing to stop them than to the dogs involved. A dog fight sounds pretty fierce, but most of the time little damage is done to either dog. But when a person get his hands into the action there is a good chance that he may come out of it with a bad bite.

If two people are present it is possible to jerk the dogs apart without danger by grabbing their back legs and flipping them over on their backs. If you are alone, and have your dog on a leash, tie him to a tree or similar holder, and pull the other dog away by hard jerks on his hind legs. But under all circumstances keep your hands away from the dogs' heads during the brawl. Even your own dog can't be trusted in the excitement of a fight.

Well, enough information has been given to keep you busy with your dog for some time. There is work connected to training a dog, but, as you see the day to day improvement in your pet's manners, you will feel highly rewarded.

Do the best you can with him — the better he minds, the more proud of him you will be. And when he is once trained, don't forget all about the subject. A little review work by master and pupil should be at least a once a week habit.

If you find that you have an unusually smart dog, or that you have a talent for training, you may become interested in following up this informal training by preparing your pet for obedience contests. These are very enjoyable, and year by year are attracting ever larger numbers of participants. If you live in a city you can no doubt find one or more groups with similar interests. If none are in your vicinity perhaps you can find enough interested dog owners to start a training club. Whether you stop your training within the scope of this book, or go on to the competitive work, I am sure that you will agree that ownership of a well mannered dog has many advantages over that of a pet which just "grows up," willful and spoiled.